CONTENTS

FOREWORD

On November 8-9, 2011, the National Defense University held a symposium entitled "Forging an American Grand Strategy: Securing a Path Through a Complex Future," at Fort Lesley J. McNair in Washington, DC. This book represents a compilation of several papers delivered at that conference. The topics discussed are relevant to the audiences of the Strategic Studies Institute, and the U.S. Army in general, students, faculty, developers of strategy, and policymakers.

Joint professional military education requires the teaching of grand strategy and the assistance such a strategy makes to the development and articulation of the *National Security Strategy*. This is the focus of much of the curriculum at all the war colleges within the Pentagon. The conference began a conversation that needs to continue because the Nation is struggling with where we are going and how we need to get there.

What is the country's grand strategy? Do we need one? If one does not exist, then in a world of complexity and globalization, what is the context that we will use to make decisions in the absence of a grand strategy that guides? How can the Nation plan in a proactive sense to be ready for the future, let alone shape one, without such a framework? The papers presented at this conference represent a sampling of the diversity of opinions on this topic. We hope that it will give the reader some issues to consider.

DOUGLAS C. LOVELACE, JR.
Director
Strategic Studies Institute and
    U.S. Army War College Press

CHAPTER 1

INTRODUCTION

Dr. Sheila R. Ronis

On November 8-9, 2011, the National Defense University (NDU), Washington, DC, held a conference entitled "Forging an American Grand Strategy: Securing a Path Through a Complex Future," which I had the privilege of chairing. For more than 2 decades, I have been studying the mechanisms and methods we use as a nation to develop and conduct grand strategy. The conversation that began at that conference needs to be further developed and continued. More importantly, we, as a nation, need to explore together the path ahead and answer questions regarding how and why we struggle with grand strategies. If developed and executed with a systemic orientation, grand strategies could help us shape our future in an ever changing and complex world.

This volume represents a compilation of some of the presentations given at the NDU conference. It also represents the great diversity of opinions regarding this subject. For more than 2 decades, it has been evident to many that the United States needs a new framework for a grand strategy, especially since the "containment" strategy of George F. Kennan that shaped U.S. policy during the Cold War is no longer relevant. But, what kind of framework do we need?

Most commonly, grand strategy is framed in the context of warfare, or at least conflict among nations. There have been exceptions, and the focus of this symposium was not on warfare or preparation for war. Our intent was to promote a discussion about the elements of and prospect for a grand strategy for America.

Over the millennia, grand strategies have evolved as the complexities of the known world grew. Rulers have created and executed grand strategies for their nations through modern times. It is possible that a 21st century grand strategy will be very different than past models since our understanding of the world has and will change our understanding of how complex systems, including nations, behave. The empowerment of individuals or small groups with new technologies and communication tools can extend beyond anything imagined outside the realm of science fiction. Other factors may come into play as well. Some would also argue that, in a democracy, it is not possible to attain the necessary consensus to craft and implement a national grand strategy in the absence of an existential threat. Recent political discourse lends some credence to that line of reasoning.

Many of us believe that an American grand strategy is not only possible, but also critical to the future of the Nation. A common strategic vision can do much to focus the attention and energies of the Nation toward a common good. In a recently published article, Dr. Anne-Marie Slaughter, formerly the Director of Policy Planning at the Department of State, succinctly described the need for a grand strategy or, to use her terminology, a national strategic narrative to serve as a guide to the future. As Dr. Slaughter says:

> We need a story with a beginning, middle, and projected happy ending that will transcend our political divisions, orient us as a nation, and give us both a common direction and the confidence and commitment to get to our destination.

During recent years, the U.S. Government has generated a plethora of strategies and strategic plans, with most aimed at some aspect of security — national, economic, space, cyber, energy — the list continues to expand. It appears clear that none of these strategies, whether separately or combined, gets to the objective succinctly identified by Dr. Slaughter — "a story with a beginning, middle, and projected happy ending that will transcend our political divisions, orient us as a nation. . . ." That storyline, with associated ways and means, is the basis for an American grand strategy. Our goals with this symposium were to help illuminate that path to the future and, along the way, pose and answer a range of fundamental questions.

- What is grand strategy?
- What lessons does history offer to today's strategists?
- Is a national grand strategy possible in today's world of complexity and divisive political turmoil?
- What is the appropriate role of the President, the Congress, the Departments of State and Defense, and the private sector in developing, supporting, and sustaining America's grand strategy?
- What system or processes are necessary to produce a U.S. grand strategy?
- What is the role of strategic foresight in developing and implementing grand strategy?
- What are the requirements for intelligence to serve national grand strategy?
- How should we educate today's and tomorrow's leaders to think strategically and to develop the necessary skills to develop and execute grand strategy?

- What are, or should be, the connections between an American grand strategy and the various national defense and security strategy documents? How can we improve those connections?

In my work with the Project on National Security Reform, I chaired the Vision Working Group. We found a need to establish a grand strategy development capability within the Executive Office of the President.

The *National Security Strategy* is the closest published document that represents a comprehensive discussion of where the country is going and what it wants to accomplish. Published by The White House from time to time, it is neither sufficiently long term nor a true strategy that links resources with objectives over time. It represents, at best, a list of aspirational goals by an administration. In a world of increasing complexity, the United States should consider long-term, whole-of-government thinking and planning. Other countries have established such a set of capabilities within the heart of their governments at the highest levels, so why not the United States in the White House?

My journey began about 20 years ago when, as a strategic management consultant to the private sector, I had an opportunity to work with the U.S. Army War College in Carlisle, Pennsylvania. When I read the U.S. *National Security Strategy* for the first time, I assumed it was a subset of a larger national "grand strategy." But, I was wrong. That summer, I realized for the first time that the United States was not developing long-term, whole-of-government grand strategies at all.

As a strategic management professor and a practitioner, I thought it was very odd that, for decades, the private sector has routinely used management tools such as forecasting, scenario based planning, strategic visioning, political and economic risk assessments, and so on, but the U.S. Government, especially in a whole-of-government way, rarely, if ever, uses such tools, though sometimes those tools are used in pockets—in specific agencies or departments.

The complex systems of the world need to have their characteristics identified, discussed, and used as a framework for the development of grand strategy. Probably the most important characteristic is that complex systems cannot be controlled—at best, they can be influenced. The systems can only be influenced if understood intimately.

A White House Center needs to be formed as a learning organization to support whatever national security structure is in place in the United States. The Center would be created to learn, analyze, assess, and synthesize risk, foresight, and the development of "grand strategy" across the government.

One of the Vision Working Group findings included the need to synthesize "all of government" solutions to complex system issues and problems, and sometimes "all of society." The only successful way to do that is to learn about the system issues and couple those with foresight tools such as Delphi techniques and risk assessment. These enable the development of scenarios for planning and ultimately the ability to develop "grand strategies." We also found that the United States needs to systematically use these tools and processes to improve decisionmaking and create mechanisms for that to happen at the whole-of-government level—at the level of the President—and that requires context and synthesis. It also requires breaking down the stovepipes of government so they can work together effectively.

Questions asked should be: What mechanisms should the U.S. Government develop to improve the Nation's ability to plan in a whole-of-government way for its future — to be better prepared for a future that will be very different from its past? What kinds of grand strategies need to be developed? Perhaps we should answer such questions as

- How do we get out of debt?
- How do we develop energy strategies to move away from fossil fuels that keep us dependent on unstable places in the world?
- How will we find the clean energy sources for a world of seven billion people that will stop and reverse global warming?
- How do we establish true peace in the Middle East?
- How do we engage permanent solutions for problematic countries, from Iraq and Afghanistan to North Korea?
- How do we stem the cyber security threats and acts of war in cyberspace from China and Russia?

These are the kinds of questions that were explored and, in the future, will need to be answered as the Nation learns to think about grand strategy capability in the world of the 21st century.

The NDU conference proceedings included Panel One, chaired by Dr. Nicholas Rostow, which discussed, "What is Grand Strategy? How Should We Develop It? What Should It Look Like?" Panels members included Ambassador Robin Raphel, Dr. Steven

Meyer, Colonel Mark "Puck" Mykleby, and Captain Wayne Porter. Panel Two, chaired by Dr. Audrey Kurth Cronin, explored the "Historical Grand Strategies and Lessons for Today." Sitting on the panel were Dr. Williamson Murray, Dr. Benjamin Franklin Cooling, and Professor Hew Strachan. Panel Three explored the question, "What is the Role of Intelligence in Supporting a Successful Grand Strategy?" Chaired by Dr. Roger George, the panel consisted of Rear Admiral Elizabeth Train, Mr. Paul Batchelor, and Dr. Matthew J. Burrows. Panel Four consisted of Dr. Hans Binnendijk and Mr. Frank Hoffman, who commented on "Strategy Overviews." Panel Four, chaired by Dr. Warren Fishbein, discussed "Grand Strategy Needs Foresight and Vision." Panel Four members were Mr. Jerome Glenn, Ms. Patricia (Patti) Morrissey, Dr. Allen Miller, and Colonel Christopher Holshek. Dr. Miller's remarks are included in this work. Panel Five, "Educating Strategists," was chaired by Colonel Greg Schultz and included Dr. Cynthia Watson, Dr. Richard Immerman, and Dr. Matthew Connelly. Finally, Panel Six, chaired by Dr. Louise Diamond, included Dr. Kristin Lord, Mr. Robert Polk, Mr. Patrick Doherty and Mr. Evan Faber. Both Bob Polk and Evan Faber's comments are included.

Sheila R. Ronis, Conference Chair
Walsh College, Troy, Michigan
May 14, 2013

CHAPTER 2

GRAND STRATEGY

Professor Leon S. Fuerth

Using complexity as a guide for thinking, this is my definition of strategy: "Any strategy is a plan for imposing a predetermined outcome on a complex system." It would be interesting to debate whether that definition is sufficient to be both precise and also sufficiently elastic to take care of all the "for instances" and practical examples, but I think it is.

A strategy has certain characteristics. It needs to be comprehensive, meaning that it purports to solve the problems of an entire set of issues. It needs to be durable enough to last until completion. It should not be susceptible to disastrous failure, in the almost certain event that it encounters conditions not foreseen in its premises.

The modifier "grand" is extremely vague, but it does convey a sense that grand strategy sits at the apex of all other plans and tactics, which should be regarded as tributary. That means that it will encompass the entire range of actions that may be required for execution: from maneuvers to tactics to battles to campaigns and upwards. Grand strategy is more than the sum of parts. It is the high ground from which all of the parts and all of their interactions can be thought through and employed as overall guidance for action.

It is not clear that grand strategies are really available. Complexity theory raises some interesting questions about this at a basic level, since we know that any action designed to solve a problem in a complex system simply causes the problem to mutate. So anyone who thinks that a grand strategy ends with a victory march needs to re-read history: to see it as a continuum in which every victory march leads on to the next set of problems with which we have to deal.

Grand strategy is definitely a narrative shared in the minds of those who lead and those who follow. The problem with that description is that it does not go far enough. Fairy tales are also narratives, and we have had rather a lot of fairy tales masquerading as grand strategies, in which the common denominator is "something for nothing." Allow me to name a few: J-curves; Laffer curves; self-correcting stock markets; eliminating the national debt by slashing taxes; growing jobs by handing out free money; revenue neutrality; the compatibility of free trade with growth strategies as practiced in Japan and China; the guaranteed existence of the American middle class; globalization lifts all ships; debt does not matter; manufacturing does not count; the trade deficit is irrelevant; subprime mortgages are secure stores of value; risk has been conquered; derivatives are safe; and the prize specimen: American exceptionalism — the attitude that the Creator is cutting us some slack because we are better than anybody else and deserve it, and that we are therefore immune from paying the consequences for things we ought to do for ourselves but, for some reason, have not.

Grand strategy requires time to be played out, and we are an impatient people, with political institutions to match. There cannot be any such thing as a fully operational grand strategy in a 2-year period. If a presidential term is 4 years, the first year is spent getting settled, and the final year is spent obsessing about being re-elected, which leaves 2 years in the middle where everyone is more or less organized around what they have found to be the central themes of the administration, which may or may not be the themes that got the administration elected in the first place.

Moreover, there cannot be a grand strategy without the capacity for strategic behavior; there can be no capacity for strategic behavior without foresight; and there can be no useful foresight without the discipline of constant reference to the facts as they materialize, rather than the facts as they were once imagined. So, finally, we come to our present predicament. I was recently at a conference put on by the U.S. Agency for International Development (USAID) to look at foresight and planning. I listened to the USAID personnel talk about what they wanted to do in the world, and finally had to remind them that, in our own country, we are presently unable to do for ourselves what they would recommend for others.

Nevertheless, the United States actually does have a grand strategy, framed by the Founding Fathers, no less. The American grand strategy was and is to have a republic ruled by its citizens through representative institutions. That is the strategy. Its objective is for citizens to remain free, rather than to default to subordination by entitled and inherited power, which — as the Founders well understood — had been the lot of all peoples throughout all history in all places previously.

You may remember Benjamin Franklin's response to a question that was put to him as he emerged from one of the discussions at the Constitutional Convention. The question was: "What have we got?" His answer was: "A Republic, if you can keep it." Everything else in American history is a continuing response to that open-ended challenge. This—the struggle to keep a republic—is the imperative behind the decisions we have made about the wars that we have fought. It is a constant factor in the organization of our domestic politics.

Right now, in the "Occupy Wall Street" movement, that question is again present. We may have disagreements about the rights of demonstrators to occupy public spaces and displace normal street traffic indefinitely, but the issue these people are raising goes to the heart of the American grand strategy. They are asking whether the 99 percent can consider themselves masters of a country mainly owned by the 1 percent. It is not a problem to design a country where 99 percent of the people are governed to suit the preferences of the remaining 1 percent. That has been done over and over again. The point of the American Revolution was that it accepted the unique challenge of designing a system that could sustain itself the other way around.

This raises the question of the tactical battles that need to be fought and won to ensure America's grand strategy continues to be operational. Let me identify a few of the push-pins in that battle map:

- We have to find a way to put politics back into proportion with the needs of the country.
- We have to cut the big banks down to size. No more masters of the universe.
- We have to cut the media empires down to size.
- We have to cut campaign spending down to size.
- We have to learn how to educate the public for engaged citizenship.

- We have to prepare our citizens with skills suited for an exceedingly competitive and essentially remorseless economic world.
- We have to fix our infrastructure. It is more important than buying our beer, our lawn furniture, and our cosmetics; it is even more important than buying computer games. It is more important than the totality of all the frivolous things that we have wasted resources on for almost 50 years now.
- We have to address climate change.
- We have to restore the concept of social burden sharing as a working principle in government.

American grand strategy inescapably includes moral values. I know that grand strategy, as taught by theoreticians, is likely to be reduced to its "scientific foundations." I have been around for a long time now, and I do not think it is possible to have an American grand strategy that is merely a theoretical construct. It needs to be an assertion of a moral principle that Americans can get behind and support, no matter how difficult that may be, given our diversity.

You might ask: "Where is national defense in this expanded concept of national security and grand strategy?" National **defense** is always fundamental, and it depends upon an honest (not a wishful) appraisal of the kind of world that we actually live in and of the kind of enemies with which we actually deal. But national **security** is a much larger concept than national defense in narrowly defined, physical terms. When you are talking about a grand strategy for America, national security only begins at the level of physical survival but does not end there. It extends to the preservation of our way of life, for ourselves in our own time, and then for posterity.

Moreover, especially in our time, grand strategy is acquiring even larger dimensions. The physical and moral survival of our Nation has become intertwined with the physical and moral survival of the civilization in which we exist, and beyond that, it even becomes a question of the survival of the human species. What does the idea of a "global" civilization mean? Is there really a civilization that is the common property of all of us? There is no better starting place for defining the civilizational dimension of grand strategy than the Four Freedoms articulated in the Atlantic Charter: freedom of speech; freedom of worship; freedom from want; and freedom from fear. Win and keep these, and everything else you might add to that list follows. Lose them, and all else that you might think of that needs to be on that list will also be lost.

We should remember that the Four Freedoms were not produced in a vacuum: they were produced in the middle of a titanic struggle, where the issues of national survival and of our ability to shape our own future were in doubt. One of the interesting features of our particular moment in time is that we can actually accomplish the objectives of the Four Freedoms. For the first time in human history, these things are not utopian or merely aspirational. They are organizational; they are the ongoing and prospective products of technologies that are already here or almost already here. They are also responses to an inextinguishable will among all peoples: a spirit that is manifesting itself right at this moment in the form of demands in every part of the globe for dignity and freedom.

This takes us back to the starting point: the capacity of the United States itself to manage its own grand strategy — a strategy of self-government by a free people in the presence of extremely complex economic, security, and political issues. Here, in addition to the questions posed by substantive solutions, I think you are still left with another that is under-recognized: the challenge of assuring competent response by the institutions of representative government.

If you look at the systems that we rely upon to move government forward, you find that the Constitution itself is as solid a rock as ever. However, the institutions and practices that we have built over the last several centuries need to be reexamined because they are very severely challenged in our time by the accelerating velocity and complexity of life. We cannot adequately deal with today's problems because our existing institutions demand that complex challenges be fragmented and oversimplified. We cannot assemble information fast enough and coherently enough. We cannot design complex policy options to deal with complex issues on the ground. We cannot execute such options coherently across the government.

The good news, however, is that we can design practical methods to improve the capacity of governance. I, like others here today, am particularly focused on ways to do this. My approaches are called Forward Engagement and Anticipatory Governance. I have spent a decade developing these methods. These ideas, like those developed by my colleagues, begin with the idea that we need to—and we *can*—blend long-range foresight into the policy process.

There is nothing magical about foresight: it is a stream of a specific kind of information that can be encouraged and organized. There is no reason why there should be a continued gap between those who think in long-range terms and those who make policy decisions. While you cannot transform long-range thinkers into political operatives and you cannot make political operatives into long-range thinkers, you can certainly find ways to introduce them to each other, and you can find ways to cross-influence their perspectives on the world. It does not require rocket science to figure out how to do it.

We also need to find ways to meld available resources so that they can be effectively brought to bear on our goals. The Department of Defense (DoD) has been moving ahead for decades to integrate, mesh, and make coherent the total effect of the weapons, strategies, and means of operations we have at our disposal. We need to carry that effort over into the civilian branch of government and begin to think in terms of what is often called "whole-of-government" operations. No matter how the debt "crisis" works out, American policy will be operating in straightened circumstances. No agency of government can carry out its mission in isolation. Reality demands that the use of our resources be orchestrated across the full range of government, regardless of formal, institutional boundaries. The means exist to improve our capacity to operate in this more seamless, more networked fashion.

We need to start applying some form of systematic feedback to give us the ability to monitor the consequences of the actions we take. We need to identify, as part of every policy, what its characteristics in operation are supposed to be and we need a system to follow that up with regular assessments, in order to generate opportunities to adapt our practices in light of experience. We have no such system. Any policy — even one that might be perfect at the time it is promulgated — inevitably loses traction. We too often learn of this only after there has been a disaster or a terrible loss of some kind, and only then do we try to diagnose what went wrong. Typically, what went wrong is that we were not auditing the policy for results.

We can improve the ability of government to think long range, to act comprehensively across jurisdictional lines, to keep track of the consequences of its actions, and to modify what it does in the light of the actual facts. I believe that it is within the power of a sitting President—without new law, without new appropriations, using customary authorities—to improve the way the system works in the White House, and from there to have an impact on the way in which the entire executive branch operates. I have vetted these ideas repeatedly in private discussions and working groups, drawing upon the expertise of seasoned veterans of the policy world and of outside experts. This process convinces me that it is feasible to upgrade critical systems in the executive branch by means of initiatives that can be implemented swiftly and efficiently, using existing presidential authorities.

I also believe it is possible to come up with a parallel form of discourse for the Congress. The form we now have is the line-item budget. It is the language of the counting room, where the subject is the balance sheet. The form of discourse we need is "management to mission," in which the budget can be understood in terms of the effects it is supposed to produce, and in which the effects are measured across the capacities of government, rather than tested for each and every one of a myriad number of government activities by a correspondingly myriad number of congressional oversight committees. That, of course, is a shift of approach that only the Congress can accept for itself, but it is do-able: far more a question of political will, than of design.

Finally, I want to loop back to the question of the moral dimension of grand strategy. Recently, Chinese authorities decided that one of China's leading dissidents (and poets) is a tax evader. They presented him with an enormous tax bill (about the equivalent of $2.4 million) and ordered him to pay it within 15 days or go back to prison. Imagine the surprise of the security apparatus when, within 1 week, 18,829 persons spontaneously contributed money to pay the fine. Funds flooded in by mail order, and even after the artist's micro-blog was shut down, people began traveling to his studio and throwing money over the walls. We can call that Tiananmen, Mod 2.

What this demonstrates, taken in the context of what we are seeing in the Middle East and what we see practically everywhere else in the world, is that the desire for freedom is as irresistible a force as running water. You can block water, but it will find its way out. "Realists" and others debate whether democracy is a necessary component of American strategy. I think the issue works out as follows: If we decide that advocacy and action for freedom is discretionary, and even exceptional, then we basically pull away from where the world is actually attempting to go. Democracy is an inalienable part of American grand strategy. It is, moreover, a winning strategy, providing we do not lose our own way. Any grand strategy combines both plan and intent. American grand strategy must include not only a goal designed for ourselves, but also an intent to represent and to work for a future that galvanizes the hopes of myriads of others.

CHAPTER 3

EDUCATING STRATEGISTS:
SOME DISCOMFORTING CONTRADICTIONS

Dr. Cynthia A. Watson

This analysis is solely that of the author and should not be construed as policy of any U.S. Government, Department of Defense, or National Defense University agency.

This chapter reflects on the challenges facing those engaged in educating U.S. grand strategists today. Rather than engage redundantly with the other panelists, this chapter will address the internal professional military education (PME) questions that are arguably as important as the theoretical ones. Within the PME environment, a number of contradictions appear that complicate executing the mission of educating strategists. It will identify several contradictions and offer some thoughts on how to go about addressing them. Many of the points will appear most relevant for students at the senior service schools (war colleges), but they are meant as general queries about how PME is evolving at all levels, as we cross-feed students to achieve whole-of-government ideas. I am not labeling the policies as bad or good decisions, but I hope to raise people's awareness of unintended consequences in seemingly "free" additions to the programs.

The point here is not to say PME is perfect; it is far from such. The intent is to lay out the contradictions that exist in the various goals set forth for PME institutions. These are trade-offs, rather than absolutes, in the overwhelming majority of cases. As is true with any other strategic decision, the ultimate responsibility is to prioritize interests in determining the best advantage in PME for the Nation.

SEVERAL OBSERVATIONS ON PME
WELL INTO THE POST-COLD WAR WORLD

PME is a luxury that few states have been able to afford in the past, yet the ability, the dedication of time, and the commitment of money to allow military officers (and civilian counterparts, to a much lesser extent[1]) to study the lessons of the past, while engaging in "safe" risk-taking in a safe environment, is important to the nation-building of a cadre of grand strategists. While world history, as well as U.S. history, is replete with examples of officers who did not have the privilege of studying the lessons of those who faced the task of orchestrating national security strategy, "contemporary" strategists such as Generals Dwight Eisenhower, George Marshall, and David Petraeus each had the opportunity to crystallize thought when studying or teaching in a PME assignment.[2] In an era of shrinking budgets, the taxpayers and Congress increasingly look at expenditures such as PME as subject to scrutiny, but the leadership of today's professional military have passed through PME in various locations to fine tune their strategic thinking.[3]

OBSERVATIONS ON PME
20 YEARS AFTER THE COLD WAR ENDED

There are a number of competing goals for the stakeholders driving PME today. Each admirable goal, based on where its supporters sit in the community, confronts similarly admirable alternate priorities which, taken together, complicate dramatically the

PME mission. An example is the International Fellows (IF) Program, which educates officers from overseas in various U.S. PME institutions. The primary goal for the Fellows is probably to strengthen the military ties between the United States and the relevant other state while enhancing strategic relations, but this overarching goal may conflict with classroom priorities. The IF students themselves, however, may come to the United States for the sake of earning a master's degree at the senior service college level or to enhance their time with their families while learning about the United States.

The contradiction that often arises comes from the classroom-driven time constraints that a participatory seminar-based academic program confronts when a student leaves to travel around the Nation on sponsored trips to learn about the U.S. countryside, culture, and economy. While this is not an automatic problem, it may create challenges for a student, particularly where English is not the native tongue, to divide her or his time between the desires of the IF leadership and the academic requirements of the college where the IF is enrolled. This is not insurmountable but has serious implications for the IF student, the U.S. cohort in any seminar, and for the instructor trying to craft a course most appropriate to a learning environment that benefits all.

Another example is the essence of the PME system itself. The primary client, thus the funding source, for professional military education is the military from which the largest component of the student body comes. The names Industrial College of the Armed Forces, the U.S. Army War College, or the Naval War College speak to the historic and foremost focus of the institution carrying that name. In any case, the largest percentage of students comes from all the armed forces in the former case, or the Navy in the latter instance. The focus of the curriculum has been overwhelmingly tied to that focus.

As student bodies have changed, however, additional sources of students bring their interests to the institutions and add to the overall understanding of these agency or service roles in the national security community.

At the same time, these additional sources of information, most likely, also bring a desire to promote or explain their value to the national security process. While that is good for basic understanding, the curriculum and time at PME institutions operate from a zero-sum reality: The time available for education is not going to grow, thus putting more material into the time available will result in either a watering down of everything or will require the academic leadership to jettison something else. This decision is an exceptionally challenging one. The stakeholders of the institutions, those who pay to enroll their students, have an expectation that their goals will be met by the curriculum, but as more agencies' personnel are added to the mix of students, those newer sources demand at least a small portion of the curriculum. Bureaucracies tend to behave in a least common denominator methodology, thus little gets taken out of the curriculum, while more is added. This is not catastrophic, but it is definitely a contradictory trend.

A specific instance of this phenomenon is when the military services seek to educate on the use of the military tool of statecraft, while building professional understanding and networks. Civilian agency students, on the other hand, seek to understand the armed forces, other national security agencies, and various other players in the national security community but do not bring the same deployment capabilities to the table.

While the overlap between these types of capabilities does occur, there are dramatic gaps between them as well. IFs come to learn about the United States, learn values, see the Nation, and get to know peers from elsewhere. This set of students offers challenges in developing curricula that answer the desires and needs of the various stakeholders. The benefits may be tremendous to all, but for those seeking to fine tune their skills exclusively in areas most tied to their traditional field, that is less likely to occur. Broadening is often cited as the greatest benefit in PME, which is exceptionally useful for today's volatile environment, but this does not always provide the basic information transfer process that some expect from PME.

Challenges to national security are much more difficult today: as the complexity of the international environment increases, rapid fire information technology affects the decisionmaking cycle, and resource constraints accelerate. This breathtaking array of complexity argues strongly for an education that broadens student views to the widest aperture.

However, today's armed forces and other national security specialties require career development—for good, sound reasons—that may conflict with the needed breadth of thinking to address the exploding variables in the international system or to think across the spectrum of national objectives. For example, offering students closer scrutiny of some of the military planning processes so they can assume positions on joint staffs and in service staffs would be quite irrelevant to the needs of students from, for instance, the Agency for International Development or Defense Intelligence Agency.

Similarly, a quarter century after passage of the Goldwater-Nichols Act, the Services retain fairly different goals from those of civilian agencies regarding the value of joint PME. PME was originally a way to introduce individual service members to the capabilities of all the Services, while emphasizing the uniqueness of their own service, in order to help understand the uses of the national military instrument for any specified scenario when the National Command Authority deems it appropriate. The school, where a military student enrolls for a set period of time to pursue a curriculum that satisfies the learning objectives set by the J-7 as suitable "joint" for a joint duty officer, aims to educate that student to fill a designated joint billet for her/his next tour. Civilian agencies, on the other hand, hunger to understand the Department of Defense (DoD) and strategy but have different objectives and missions, such as understanding how to integrate the national security policymaking bureaucracy, rather than to accomplish a specific mission.

Some advocates have argued for sending only the brightest students to civilian educational institutions, because PME does not produce the most rigorous thinking. This idea is counter to the intent of the Goldwater-Nichols Act, which aimed at addressing PME as a portion of the reforms to the military. In the 1980s, the Congress, especially Representative Ike Skelton of Missouri, took a strong interest in pushing the PME community to address those deficiencies that prevented producing officers like Generals Marshall and Eisenhower.[4]

Additionally, military education in 2011 has multiple masters who have rather different goals in mind. The J-7 and the military side find their work governed by the Officer Professional Military Education Policy, which allows PME schools to develop curricula to achieve their responsibilities, which, in turn, will allow students to meet requirements under the Goldwater-Nichols Act for joint officer qualification. Congress has further sought additional intellectual rigor and inflicted on PME institutions a civilian credentialing process. Agencies providing civilian students are seeking to learn about the military and security missions in an era of declining funding, thus making them ready to step into individual circumstances as a better rounded U.S. representative. Generals Petraeus and H. R. McMaster both went to civilian schools (Princeton and University of North Carolina Chapel Hill, respectively) and have been cited as stating that the reason was that these civilian programs give creative thinkers a much better experience than does PME.[5]

Promoting traditional civilian graduate programs would have three serious challenges that are not true in PME institutions. A doctorate, admittedly not currently available at a PME school, would take an officer out of his/her career path for a minimum of 3 years.[6] However, few officers probably want to engage in the doctoral process as they advance in their careers.

A second issue is that most graduate programs would not have the substantive basis to provide adequate instruction on joint professional military education (JPME) topics to qualify a graduate as a joint duty officer required under Goldwater-Nichols for promotion to flag officer. Civilian institutions simply have no reason to cover those topics in their graduate programs. Third, the often less-than-subtle anti-military bias at many civilian institutions would make this a less efficacious venture than it sounds. While personal bias against the military is one aspect that still exists widely across the academy, it is manifested clearly in the lack of military studies topics, such as military history, security studies, and related fields, at U.S. graduate schools.

A tremendous challenge increasingly confronting PME is that much of the new technology and many new technology-driven pedagogies that may be used offer a new direction for educating strategists but require additional sustained funding. Increasingly, technology-driven solutions to deliver education appeal more to students than physical books or arriving at a brick and mortar school. The computers for library access or communication are not a single purchase but require replenishment on a regular cycle, thus incurring a commitment to information technology (IT) refreshment that becomes expensive over the long term. Furthermore, hard copies of anything take longer to reach the consumer—faculty and students—and run the risk of being outdated more quickly than is true of electronic delivery.

However, a commitment to the more environmentally friendly electronic age requires a sustained commitment to keeping technology up-to-date, which is an expensive commitment. This may make PME institutions rethink their priorities to allow for this constant, at least annual, refurbishment of the technology base.

Additionally, electronic resources for delivering PME come up against information assurance levels. As students prefer using electronic tablets that they may buy themselves, how does the institution prevent cyber problems from arising? The DoD has already banned "thumb drives" after apparent infiltration of the U.S. network by some adversary that may have used a thumb drive to gain access; banning students from hooking up their personal tablets to a network will make it much harder to transfer basic administrative information in an educational institution. This is not a reason to terminate the program, but it will require more time and assets by the PME institutions to establish firewalls or duplicative systems to prevent cross-contamination.

The academic community is now driven by concerns about assessments and proof of non-cross-contamination, which affect the environment for U.S. military education. But that education focuses on the measurable academic content of the program, as well as on some of the development of personal ties among students and their gaining an understanding of basic capabilities across the national security community. Academic assessment drives faculty to worry about whether learning objectives have been achieved and how to measure that achievement.

This has, arguably, brought more rigor to the PME classroom but may incur less faculty tolerance for the seminar process to develop personal ties among students than was true in the past. The pressure to measure if students have mastered the learning objectives requires more attention to developing those objectives, crafting the instruments of assessments, and taking time to digest the results. This is time taken away from faculty for developing courses or refining discussion approaches for a particular topic. New faculty especially need time to develop their courses.

THE FACULTY

PME faculty composition may lead to tension; each type of faculty brings different goals and understanding of what an institution seeks to accomplish. This can affect educating strategists, as various instructors bring their particular views into the classroom. On the one hand, each faculty member brings to the institution her/his specific benefits to the faculty mix. Uniformed faculty with tactical/operational/strategic experience worry about how well students understand the military instrument and who they may send into the field in hard-headed, fundamental ways, but they are not as interested in abstract academic arguments that may not matter outside of the classroom or a refereed journal. Agency faculty coming from the civilian part of the government also arrive with vast tactical/operational/strategic experience but are stretched thin by their agencies' challenges to keep up with operational imperatives. When they arrive at a PME institution, they often are still doing a bit of their home agency work as they challenge students to see the trade-offs in the real world challenges ahead. Both of these types of faculty are acutely sensitive to the on-the-ground experiences of their students and often spend countless hours in mentoring students because of the faculty-student bonds over various experiences in the field, especially in the post-September 11, 2001 (9/11) environment.

Title X[7] civilians, hired in greater numbers since 1989 to increase rigor and strategic thinking, often may have had prior government experience. However, some are most interested in teaching and traditional academic research, which drives them toward time away from the classroom. While all faculty are expected to teach, mentor, and engage in research and outreach, too many Title X faculty, who often arrived at PME institutions by serving in traditional academic institutions where a "publish or perish" atmosphere dominates, prefer not to grasp many of the collateral responsibilities in administration at the college, preferring instead to do research. This attitude creates tensions among the faculty. An unstated attitude implies that researchers are "better" faculty than those who are not engaged in published research in refereed journals. In fact, time spent in research may take away from time spent in classroom preparation. Publishing is no guarantee that an individual is a better seminar leader because the skills are different. Similarly, there are military and agency personnel who have engaged in research, but their contributions are too often dismissed as not being on the same level as their civilian colleagues. This is an easily remedied issue, if approached clearly and openly.

More important for any PME institution is the problem of Title X faculty doing serious research while agency and military faculty are doing the pedestrian work of mentoring, faculty advising, and other internal, less glamorous tasks. The fact that Title X faculty qualify for sabbaticals is an example. To a faculty member who has been deployed to Iraq or Afghanistan for several tours, a sabbatical is an appealing but unavailable option, since for the individual, sabbaticals are only applicable to Title X faculty who have served in their positions for 6 years. This implies a second-class status to many uniformed or agency faculty at PME schools.

More broadly, the type of activities engaged in by the faculty should answer the following questions for their employment at PME institutions: First, how do these activities affect the education mission? Second, are the effects positive or negative? Further, uniformed and agency faculty almost always are assigned to a PME institution for shorter periods than their Title X colleagues; thus, they have significantly less impact on the curriculum development, even if their practical experiences are valuable to the students. Additionally, teaching may be harder for these practitioners who come to PME institutions because their experiential skills are not necessarily appropriate to some teaching environments. Yet these individuals add a great deal to the unique curriculum of PME institutions; they add a vital portion to the educational experience **because** they have experience in the field addressing the nuts and bolts of hard strategic and operational concerns.

The efficacy of hiring traditional civilian academics as opposed to those with considerable practical policy experience is another frequent contradiction confronting PME. Many supporters of hiring traditional, "publish or perish" academics note that PME schools, under Title X hiring practices only offer renewable, nontenured positions instead of the traditional tenure system. Many people argue that this undermines the quality of the faculty who come to PME schools, since the best quality academics can command tenure, high salaries, extensive research time, little time in the classroom, and broader power over faculty governance. The PME community has tended to prefer Title X regulations, however, because they allow shorter term, but renewable, hiring to give the institutions greater flexibility, while also preventing the development of "dead wood" that many critics charge is true in traditional academic environments. Under existing conditions, PME faculty have clear-cut responsibilities that prioritize teaching, with some research, outreach, and administrative responsibilities.

Those who argue for hiring traditional academic faculty increasingly advocate a PME system that focuses more on publishing in peer-reviewed, mainline academic disciplines and journals, thus making the faculties look more like those at traditional universities. Opponents argue that the students at PME schools are not there for the same research requirements characterizing traditional academe and that the former practitioners — whether uniformed or agency — offer far more relevant challenges to the students than do abstract research-driven academics. This remains a point of tremendous difference between various people in the PME field.

The type of civilian faculty hires have other effects as well. A traditional academic develops a curricula looking at strategy in a more abstract way rather than based on current national security policies or challenges that may be more applicable to students today. The lieutenant colonel who goes to the Air War College may benefit from a curriculum with far less theory than one that pushes her/him to wrestle with a hard-to-solve practical problem about logistics in Afghanistan. Academics from traditional backgrounds assume that research helps in the classroom, but students are not always certain of any correlation, much less one between research and the quality of teaching.

Title Xs also tend toward specialization along academic disciplinary "research" lines rather than across the PME institution's broadest mission, perhaps creating artificial academic boundaries that limit student benefit. An Army Foreign Area Officer would be aware of the cultural, political, linguistic, historic, economic, and military aspects of the area into which she/he is sent because of the relevance to the mission, as has become clear in Afghanistan and Iraq. Traditional academic disciplines in the United States today rarely allow this sort of interdisciplinary work. The rigid commitments to discipline have their advantages for academics but may affect the quality of student thinking about responding to international threats.

Specialists who focus on research think in terms of their "lanes," creating a disincentive to focus on broad curricula because specialists prefer to teach where they have invested time rather than in the core curriculum. This does not mean they cannot broaden their work, but they may be reluctant to do so. Additionally, theoretical academics may not be as interested in educating students in broad grand strategy questions since they often work in extremely narrow areas of inquiry.

These are two differences between Title X and agency/military faculty that may function as PME teachers. They are not balanced, since the typically longer tenure of Title X faculty gives their ideas greater weight in curricula development and other functional aspects of PME. This imbalance argues for hiring only Title X faculty who have previous, extensive experience as military officers or civilian officials.

How students fit into the PME system is also an important issue. Many students arrive with little, if any, idea of where they will go upon completing their PME work, but the Services often appear to pay little attention to where they will post students upon completion of schooling. Agency students, on the other hand, often return to precisely the same jobs they had before studying. The lack of systematic assignments for military students relates to force needs but begs the question of whether this is a good use of assets — human and fiscal.

A student may "fill a billet" rather than be best prepared for a particular school if the service or agency has a slot allocated but unfilled at the beginning of a school period. This appears to undermine student interest and occasionally preparation. This also may affect the quality of the seminars in which the student participates.

Students' personal desires based on a need to keep children in school or a spouse in a job may trump the "logic" of a particular school's curriculum for a student's career path. In the all-volunteer force, this reality collides with an ideal vision of handpicking every entrant to PME classes around the country. The Services' desire to educate their officers may affect the mix of students in the schools. Increasingly, DoD and non-DoD civilians attend the schools with active duty personnel. While this trend may increase the civilian capacity in national security education, is it diluting the objectives of the DoD and the individual Services?

FINAL THOUGHTS

Educating strategists is a zero-sum game: The time available is finite and extraordinarily unlikely to increase for fiscal and professional reasons. Taxpayers do not want to spend more on having the force in the schoolhouse, and the career advancement of someone who spends all available time in school may be seriously undermined. Any addition to the curriculum leads to watering down of quality or removing something else, which is hard to explain to the affected stakeholder. Each and every topic has a fierce advocate who argues passionately for his/her addition to the curriculum. Faculty composition, goals, and incentives matter to the schools, to their graduates, and to the quality of teaching and research.

PME will continue to generate costs beyond salaries and the building maintenance, especially for keeping technology on the cutting edge where the DoD tries to sustain the highest quality force. No single agreed standard exists for achieving the best education for strategists, but we likely cannot achieve **everything** to the highest level in the time the taxpayer and the Services want to allocate. Educating strategists requires prioritizing objectives for PME as much as thinking great thoughts.

I do not note any one of these contradictions as a reason to terminate PME in the United States. It has inherent value, ranging from students from all agencies meeting their peers and the probable decisionmakers for the next 2 decades, to finding the best strategic thinker on Carl von Clausewitz's view of leadership. PME has many things that make it absolutely the best in the world because of the resources the United States puts into it.

The purpose of these thoughts is to point out that different parts of the U.S. national security community have different aspirations for sending students and resources into the PME community. Those aspirations may coincide, or they may be directly in contradiction. Without understanding and stating that these differences exist, we are less likely to be effective in this whole process in the years ahead at a time when the taxpayers expect us to be the best stewards of the public expenditures, be they time or money.

The PME system still works and allows many students to flourish. It is not the same as a traditional academic experience, but these students are not traditional, either. Without the opportunities that the various levels of education have, the U.S. national security community would be weaker and less useful to the Nation. It is not perfect, but it challenges them to open their minds and to produce the leadership the Nation and those of various international students in our programs need.

ENDNOTES - CHAPTER 3

1. While I will discuss civilians in various places in this chapter, the overwhelming focus is on military education for professional military officers, which falls under DoD as a part of the officer development programs. I am in no way misinterpreting the need for civilians to learn more about the military, about strategy, or about what are often called whole-of-government solutions to national security concerns, but adding the civilian sector of the government would make this topic unwieldy for a conference paper except at the most vague level of analysis.

2. General Eisenhower studied and taught simultaneously at the Army Industrial College in the mid-1930s; General Marshall taught at the U.S. Army War College in the 1920s, as well as at the Infantry School at Fort Benning, GA; and General Petraeus studied at Princeton in the 1980s after completing the Command and General Staff Officer Course at Fort Leavenworth, KS.

3. Chairman of the Joint Chiefs of Staff U.S. Army General Martin Dempsey graduated from the National War College, as did Air Force Chief of Staff General Norton Schwartz and the Combatant Commanders for Southern, Central, and European Commands, General Douglas Fraser, USAF, General James Mattis, USMC, and Admiral James Stavridis, USN, respectively. Vice Chief of the Joint Chiefs Admiral James Winnefeld and Chief of Staff of the Army General Raymond Odierno graduated from the Naval War College. General Carter Ham of the U.S. Africa Command and the Commandant of the Marine Corps General James Amos did senior service school studies at the Air War College.

4. In 2007, I presented Representative Skelton with a copy of my *Military Education* (Santa Barbara, CA: ABC Clio, 2007) in his office. He thumbed through it and then asked me whether I could seriously say that the students produced by the National War College could compete intellectually with General Marshall or General Eisenhower. I said I believed they could and explained why. He gave me a long look and concluded by saying "Well, I hope so. We need them."

5. I would argue there are countless counterarguments of officers who excelled at PME and were every bit as creative when they returned to the force. General Dempsey, National War College Class of 1996, is a prime example, as is General John Allen, USMC (National War College, 1999).

6. An exception to this is an officer pursuing her or his doctorate while serving at a Reserve Officer Training Corps (ROTC) unit as an instructor at a traditional civilian school. The assignment would be probably 3 years, which does take the officer out of the operating forces but is not seen by the Services as the same period outside of the traditional career path due to the teaching function that he/she would engage with cadets, when one teaches at the Service academies.

7. Title X refers to the portion of the U.S. Code, in this case covering the DoD, that authorizes hiring civilian faculty members for PME assignments. The shortening of the concept to Title X is a common usage within the military education community.

CHAPTER 4

EIGHT MYTHS ABOUT AMERICAN GRAND STRATEGY

Dr. Peter D. Feaver

Grand strategy appears to be the flavor of the month in the strategic community. I have planned or been invited to numerous conferences looking at the topic, and the debates on this topic are as lively as I can remember in a long time. Just recently, I gave a talk to a grand strategy conference at National Defense University on the myths that afflict the field.[1]

MYTH 1:
THE UNITED STATES CANNOT DO GRAND STRATEGY

Many critics claim that the United States is simply too disorganized to do strategy on a grand scale. In fact, we had a coherent grand strategy during the 19th century built around the Monroe Doctrine. We had a coherent grand strategy during World War II built around winning in Europe first. We had a coherent grand strategy during the Cold War built around the idea of containment.

MYTH 2:
THE UNITED STATES LOST THE ABILITY TO DO GRAND STRATEGY WHEN THE SOVIET UNION DISAPPEARED

Many critics concede we had a grand strategy during the Cold War but claim that we have not had one since. This is by far the most prevalent myth, and some of the very best in the business peddle it. In fact, we have had a coherent, bipartisan, and largely successful grand strategy from George H. W. Bush to Bill Clinton to George Bush to Barack Obama.

MYTH 3:
A GRAND STRATEGY HAS TO HAVE
A 3-SYLLABLE LABEL THAT RHYMES
WITH "AINMENT"

This gets to the heart of why you get the odd argument that we had a grand strategy during the Cold War but we have not since. When critics say that we have not had a grand strategy since the end of the Cold War, what they really mean is that we have not had a label like "containment" that enjoys widespread popularity. This is true, but trivial. In fact, since the fall of the Soviet Union, a five-pillar grand strategy has been clearly discernible.

Pillar I.

The velvet covered iron fist: The "iron fist" built a military stronger than what is needed for near-term threats to dissuade a would-be hostile rival from achieving peer status. "Velvet" accommodated major powers on issues, giving them a larger stake in the international distribution of goodies than their military strength would command to dissuade a near-peer from starting a hostile rivalry.

Pillar 2.

Make the world more like us politically by promoting the spread of democracy.

Pillar 3.

Make the world more like us economically by promoting the spread of markets and globalization.

Pillar 4.

Focus on weapons of mass destruction (WMD) proliferation to rogue states as the top tier national security threat.

Pillar 5 (added by George W. Bush).

Focus on terrorist networks of global reach inspired by militant Islamist ideologies as another top tier national security threat, i.e., equal to WMD in the hands of rogue states. The nexus of Pillars 4 and 5 is the *ne plus ultra* threat.

No administration described the strategy in exactly these terms. Every President succumbed to the political temptation to produce differentiation and especially to describe one's own actions as a bold new departure from the "failed" efforts of his predecessor. Yet, a fair-minded reading of the core governmental white papers on strategy, especially the *National Security Strategy* reports prepared by each administration, as well as the central policy efforts each administration pursued, reveals a broad 20-year pattern of continuity.

All post-Cold War Presidents championed the first four pillars. The last two Presidents (Bush and Obama) adopted the last two pillars. The major grand strategic moves of the period derive from one or more of these pillars: e.g., the outreach to India derives from Pillar 1, the invasion of Iraq derives from Pillars 4 and 5, and so on.

Obama campaigned as if he was going to make a grand strategic innovation by adding a 6th pillar: elevating climate change to be equal to WMD and terrorism. But he chose to do health care instead.

MYTH 4:
MAYBE WE HAD GRAND STRATEGIES, BUT THEY WERE FOLLIES

Some critics say that maybe the United States has tried grand strategies, but we are just not good at it. In fact, all of the grand strategies I have mentioned were largely successful. I defy you to identify a great power that has had a better 230+-year run, or a better 100-year run, or a better 50-year run. Maybe we could have an interesting debate about whether some countries have had a better 20-year run. Perhaps Prussia under Bismarck had a better 20 years, though the period afterwards rather took the luster off the earlier achievements. In the era of U.S. sole-superpowerdom, a number of near-great powers have thrived by free-riding on the public goods provided by the United States.

Now I concede that China has had a better last 3 years or so than the United States has had. But despite the bluff and bluster from Beijing, it is clear that Chinese leaders understand the very daunting challenges they face. Betting against America for the medium to long run boosts one's speaker's fees, but it otherwise has not been validated by history.

As great powers go, we have a remarkably good track record. Perhaps you will argue we have just been lucky. I think the capacity to select satisfactory grand strategies and to refine those strategies as circumstances dictate is part of the story.

MYTH 5:
A GRAND STRATEGY ONLY EXISTS IF IT COMMANDS SUCH A DOMINANT CONSENSUS AS TO END ALL POLITICS AT THE WATER'S EDGE

If stopping at the water's edge means parties do not have strong disagreements about foreign policy ends and means and do not seek political advantage from foreign policy maneuvers, then I do not know of a period when this happened in U.S. history. A large part of the confusion about today's grand strategy is due to sloppy historical understanding of the Cold War grand strategy. Containment was coherent enough as an overarching grand strategy to be recognizably operative from 1947-89. But during that period, that left room for deeply divisive debates about:
- The need to defend the Korean peninsula,
- The need to prevent falling dominos in Southeast Asia,
- The possibility and desirability of splitting the Soviet pact,
- The mix of confrontation and *détente*,
- The adequacy of arms control, and
- The requirements of nuclear deterrence.

The point is that grand strategies have lots of subordinate debates. We tend to exaggerate the strategic consensus during the Cold War and the strategic dissensus during the post-Cold War.

MYTH 6:
A GRAND STRATEGY HAS TO BE
FORWARD-LOOKING

On the contrary, grand strategies tend to be backward-looking. If generals prepare to fight the last war, grand strategists prepare to avoid fighting the last war. Thus, containment was designed to confront the Soviet Challenge while avoiding another global war like World War II. The post-Cold War grand strategy has been designed to deal with the challenges we face today while avoiding another cold war (i.e., another rivalry where our global interests are challenged by a hostile peer competitor). Even Bush's refinement of the post-Cold War strategy, elevating the threat posed by militant Islamism, had a heavy dollop of backward-looking "never again" to it.

Of course, any successful grand strategy must also address the evolving and future strategic environment. Thus, containment had to adjust to post-colonialism and the Sino-Soviet split. The Bush global war on terror (GWOT) was unusually forward-looking, with its emphasis on promoting political and economic liberty in the broader Middle East and its willingness to contemplate short-term costs to achieve long-term benefits.

But most grand strategies begin with a look backward before they look forward. To the extent that we are starting a fundamental debate about our grand strategy today, it is probably out of a desire to avoid another GWOT, which is a high cost, high operations tempo conflict with a dispersed global footprint.

Myth 7:
A GRAND STRATEGY REQUIRES
AN EXISTENTIAL THREAT

It may be easier to describe the grand strategy when there is an overarching existential threat to concentrate the mind. But as the post-Cold War has shown, it is possible to have a coherent grand strategy even when the threats are dispersed and less than existential.

The Cold War was not a time when everything was simple, or when everyone knew priorities, or when everyone agreed on the threat. It sure wasn't "a time of great stability and security unlike these really dangerous times today" — a curious view that I hear most often from students who never lived through the Cold War era. But it was a time when the much more obvious — and by the late-1950s, possibly existential — threat posed by the nuclear confrontation overlaid on top of a global ideological contest with the Soviet Union circumscribed strategic thinking in a way that is not the case today. Compared to the Cold War period, we have more slack in our security environment, and that introduces a certain amount of indeterminacy in the strategic debate.

MYTH 8:
ONLY BIG GRAND STRATEGY SHIFTS MATTER

There is vastly more continuity than change between Obama and his predecessors. As you move up the ladder from rhetoric to policy and to strategy, the higher the level, the more this is true. But over time, the small changes can be significant, like a one-degree shift in the vector of an aircraft carrier over a 1,000-mile voyage.

So the comparatively small changes—small compared to the outsized rhetoric of the 2008 campaign—could, over time, be quite consequential. Obama has made some very consequential and risky bets. If they do not pay out, they could force a reconsideration of our grand strategy. Indeed, the ferment in the strategic community about grand strategy suggests that such a reconsideration is well underway.

ENDNOTES - CHAPTER 4

1. Posted by Peter Feaver on Wednesday, November 23, 2011, 11:47 AM, on Shadow Government and first delivered at the National Defense University Conference entitled "Forging an American Grand Strategy" held in Washington, DC, on November 8-9, 2011.

CHAPTER 5

DEPARTMENT OF HOMELAND SECURITY APPROACH TO STRATEGY

Dr. Allen S. Miller

This presentation covers the Department of Homeland Security (DHS) systems approach to risk informing strategy, how risk assessment processes interact with foresight, and how these processes may be applied to the development of an American grand strategy.

The DHS was created in 2003. At that time, the focus of the Department was on preventing terrorist attacks. Since then, the focus has been broadened to include natural and accidental hazards. From the beginning, DHS was thrust into the world of homeland security strategy development. The first *National Strategy for Homeland Security* and many subsequent national and department level documents identified risk assessment and risk management as the fundamental approach to addressing the challenges of securing the homeland. The Nation and DHS recognized that they could not secure everything, everywhere, all the time, and certainly would not be able to provide complete security from the vast and diverse set of threats and hazards we continually face.

In 2007, DHS created the Office of Risk Management and Analysis (ORMA) and charged that Office with developing an integrated approach to homeland security risk management. The ORMA immediately convened a risk steering committee (RSC) consisting of members from across the offices and components of DHS. The DHS RSC developed a vision that included integration across the many organizations that make up the homeland security enterprise, integration across risk assessments from numerous perspectives, and integration across levels of strategies designed to manage homeland security risks. Integration of organizations, risk assessments, and risk management strategies is recognized as the way to improve and provide homeland security in a unified manner.

Organizations with a role, responsibility, or contribution to homeland security include DHS and its federal partners, as well as our state, local, territorial, tribal, private sector, and international partners. These organizations are viewed as components of a system of organizations that make up the homeland security enterprise. Furthermore, as with any system, it is critical that one understand the relationships, the interactions, and the interdependencies among the components, such that the enterprise can leverage the synergies of the components that make up the system. DHS recognized that homeland security was not going to be achieved by any one organization, but by the collective unified efforts of many organizations.

Furthermore, organizations in the homeland security enterprise assess homeland security risks from multiple and various perspectives. Risk is generally defined as a function of likelihood and consequences, or a function of threats, vulnerabilities, and consequences of an unwanted outcome resulting from an incident, event, or occurrence. Each organization has a different role, responsibility, or contribution and therefore assesses homeland security risks from different perspectives. In some cases, an organization will assess risk from a particular threat or hazard perspective. For example, the DHS Domestic Nuclear Detection Office assesses nuclear and radiological risks for the purpose of improving our capability to detect and report on such activity. In other cases, organizations assess risk from a mission perspective. For example, the Federal Emergency Management Agency, a federal agency charged with building and supporting the Nation's emergency management system, assesses risks to inform national preparedness and resilience. In other cases, organizations assess risk from a domain perspective. For example, the Transportation Security Administration assesses risk in the air domain and the Coast Guard in the maritime domain. Lastly, there are times when organizations assess risk from a functional perspective. For example, DHS assesses risks associated with security screening and domain awareness functions that cut across multiple DHS organizations.

In addition to assessing risk, the organizations that make up the homeland security enterprise also develop strategies to manage homeland security. Strategies in general, either implicitly or explicitly, describe objectives, methods to achieve those objectives, and the resources required to implement. In senior service college language, it is: ends, ways, and means. National level strategies serve to provide overarching goals or objectives for the Nation and provide the context for supporting strategies to be developed and implemented by departments, agencies, and their components. For example, there are national level strategies, supported by DHS level strategies, further supported by DHS cross-component strategies and DHS component strategies. The connectivity across independent but complementary strategies facilitates a unified approach to securing the homeland.

There are obviously many combinations of ways one can integrate organizations, assessments, and strategies. Furthermore, as the organizations and the risks we face as a Nation continuously evolve, the security strategies must also evolve. Therefore, continuous coordination and collaboration on our independent but supportive assessments and strategies to achieve desired and shared objectives is a significant and ongoing challenge for DHS integrated risk management (IRM).

How does this DHS view of IRM intersect with foresight? All risk assessments and strategies, either implicitly or explicitly, include a temporal aspect. They may be developed and implemented for short-term, medium-term, or long-term time horizons. This temporal aspect is one intersection between risk assessment and foresight. Risk can be assessed for the current environment, as well as for short-term, medium-term, or long-term time horizons. Risk is generally defined as the potential for an unwanted outcome resulting from an incident, event, or occurrence, as determined by its likelihood and the associated consequences. Foresight is generally defined as the disciplined analysis of alternative futures. Therefore, risk assessments on today's security environment can set the foundation from which to conduct a foresight analysis to identify potential alternative security futures. Each of those alternative security futures can then be further assessed from a risk perspective. Collectively, developing information about today's risk, information about alternative security futures, and information about risk associated with those alternative security futures can inform a path forward for an organization and the Nation.

Another intersection between risk assessment and foresight is the area of opportunity analysis. Assessing the likelihood of opportunities and the consequences of deciding whether to engage in them is another form of risk information needed to forge a path forward for an organization or the Nation.

The following example demonstrates how the interaction among risk and opportunity assessments, foresight, and temporal aspects could interact. One could assess the year 2012 to determine the relationships, interactions, interdependencies, and synergies to be gained from the organizations in 2012; assess the risks we face in 2012; and assess the strategies those organizations have in place to address those risks. Using that as a foundation, engage foresight organizations to define alternative futures for 2025. The organizations in 2025 may have different relationships, interactions, interdependencies, and synergies. In 2025, we may be expecting very different risks and may need a very different set of strategies to manage those risks. Similar to assessing risks we may face and developing strategies to address those risks, we must also assess the opportunities we may be given and address strategies to manage those opportunities. An analysis of the likelihood of opportunities and an analysis of the consequences of engaging or not engaging in the opportunity are as critical as the analysis of the risk.

From an American grand strategy perspective, anything the Nation can do to better understand the system of interacting organizations and to improve the way we assess our risks and opportunities for the current security environment, as well as alternative future environments, significantly strengthens the ability of the Nation to function in a unified manner into the future. These kinds of analyses and assessments can provide invaluable information for planning and decisionmaking over any time horizon the Nation values. Engaging in analysis to support strategy development helps us learn something about where we have been as a Nation, learn something about where we are currently as a Nation, learn something about alternatives for the future, and become increasingly anticipatory in the way we govern our Nation and shape the world in which we will live.

There are at least three questions worthy of consideration going forward. First, what organization should lead, and which organizations should contribute to the development of the next American grand strategy? Second, how do we educate more people to engage in critical thinking about strategic thinking at the national level? Outside of the DoD, few have the opportunity for the kind of education offered at the National Defense University and the other senior service colleges. Third, how can the Nation apply more rigorous analysis to foresight and opportunity, similar to what we do for risk and security analysis, and use the resulting information to develop strategies that shape the future and facilitate anticipatory governance?

CHAPTER 6

FORGING GRAND STRATEGY:
THE PRESIDENT'S ROLE

Dr. David M. Abshire

In opening this conference, National Defense University President Vice Admiral Anne Rondeau offered a sobering observation: The United States has been searching for a grand strategy since the fall of the Berlin Wall in 1989.

Leading scholars in the field have provided a framework through which the rest of us can approach this challenge. Leon Fuerth has called for better ways to look at long-term strategic planning. Dr. Anne-Marie Slaughter has endorsed the idea that such planning should produce a grand strategy. Captain Wayne Porter and Colonel Mark Mykleby, associates of former Chairman of the Joint Chiefs Admiral Mike Mullen, have called for a long-term strategic narrative to tell the story of our Nation into the future. Our mission is to explore potential building blocks and roadmaps for this narrative and to consider possible structures for such a grand strategy. My contribution to the discussion is the application of the lessons of history, particularly to the role of the Chief Executive as Grand Strategist.

The President is empowered by Article II of the Constitution as a very powerful commander in chief. Article I retains for Congress the right to declare war, but war has been declared only five times in American history. Despite periodic objections from Congress, the President has exercised his power to command in over 125 other military actions. But the clear scope of this power only extends to military strategy. The President cannot simply command the acceptance of a long-term grand strategy by Congress or the public. He must resort to what the late Dean of Presidential Historians Richard Neustadt called the "Power of Persuasion." To become "Grand Strategist in Chief," the President must first become "Persuader in Chief." It is our challenge to persuade the Persuader in Chief of the necessity of a long-term grand strategy and to offer him a practical pathway to it. Today, that means convincing the current President that this long-term consensus-building approach can help end the political civil war in Washington.

Arguments against the possibility of developing any strategic consensus are based on the mistaken belief that our current post-Cold War environment lacks the national uniting force of an easily identified opponent or cause: an Adolf Hitler, Pearl Harbor, or Joseph Stalin. Especially since the elimination of Osama bin Laden, it is common to hear that there is no such threat to our Nation today. WRONG. The threat is the potential decline of America as a leading global power. History makes clear that the seeds of decline are always sown within the nation—from Athens and Rome through the British Empire and Japanese economic power. American decline will be no different. It will be the result of diminishing economic strength and competitiveness, not global politics. A strong domestic economy is the engine of national success. Today, the pistons of our national power are out of alignment, and our engine has a serious misfire. If we do not fix this, America's role in the world will wane, and the American dream will end.

For these reasons, I believe the threat to the Nation is as great today as in 1787, 1861, 1941, and at the dawn of the Cold War. Accepting this urgency, the question then is how to convince the Chief Executive, as well as Congress, that there can be a consensus-building, long-term, bipartisan narrative to lead the Nation back to its full potential: domestically sound, internationally strong, and globally competitive.

WHAT IS STRATEGY?

The word strategy is derived from *strategos*, the Greek word for generalship. *Webster's Dictionary* says strategy is the process of ensuring the enemy is joined in combat under advantageous conditions. The Greeks understood strategy as the process of using multiple stratagems — initiative, agility, flexibility, and especially deception — to upset an opponent's equilibrium. Strategy involves developing, revising, and adapting pathways to achieve longer-term goals, while ensuring a reasoned relationship exists between the means and the ends. Strategy depends on vision, innovation, resiliency, and timing. In contrast to an attrition approach, which is reactive and based on brute force, strategy always seeks, through new invention, tactics, or mobility, to seize and retain the initiative. Most important, strategy is a **process** to achieve certain ends, the opposite of a fixed plan of specific means to those ends.

The strategic process is built on three principles of classical Greek strategy, all still applicable today. The first is Unity of Effort. The second is, as Herodotus put it, Freedom of Action, which offers the chance for agility and deception to upset an opponent's equilibrium. The third is Proportionality. The classic case of disproportionality was recounted by Thucydides, when, against the advice of Pericles, Athens attacked Syracuse, an unnecessary over-extension of limited resources.

Grand strategy is strategy writ large, extended in scope, perspective, purpose, and time frame. It is also built around three pillars. First, that it actually be a strategy rather than just a plan; that it incorporate the three core principles and the basic characteristics of the strategic process. Second, that it be long-term and comprehensive; that it derive from a nation's character, incorporating any exceptional national qualities, and be grounded in the strength of a sound domestic economy where all the economic pistons are firing in order. Third, that it be grounded in what Walter Lippmann called a Public Philosophy; that it be something all Americans can understand and embrace, and in which they can participate. This last characteristic makes grand strategy the purview of Presidents. Only the President, as Persuader in Chief, can turn a strategic concept into a true public strategy.

The ultimate aim of strategy is to shape the environment over the long term rather than being slave to the short-term demands of externalities. The ultimate aim of grand strategy must be to do this on a national and global basis, to leverage innate strengths and resources, to get all our pistons firing together, to keep our focus above and beyond the crises we face on a daily basis, and thereby to reclaim our mantle of global leadership.

PAST PRESIDENTS AS
GRAND STRATEGY MAKERS

The question at hand is whether America and an American President can create or foster a grand strategy, or as Michael Lind put it so well in *The American*

Way of Strategy, a way "to defend the American way of life by means that do not endanger the American way of life." History says yes, it can be done in the future because it has been done in the past. The lessons of the Presidents who have been successful grand strategists are there to persuade our current and future Presidents of the way ahead.

Our first President, General George Washington, understood that being Commander in Chief meant being Strategist in Chief as well. Soon after assuming office, he laid down a national strategy influenced by his Treasury Secretary, Alexander Hamilton. The new Republic faced a depression at home and a lack of creditworthiness abroad because each individual state had issued its own debt to finance the Revolution, and some were not honoring their obligations. The new administration consolidated state debt and set up the first national bank. This emphasis on credit and debt management fostered national prosperity and provided a foundation for rapid economic expansion.

As emphasized in his Farewell Address, Washington also opposed foreign entanglements. President James Monroe, with his Secretary of State, future President John Quincy Adams, built on this idea with the Monroe Doctrine. If Washington had warned that we should stay out of Europe, then Monroe warned Europeans to stay out of America.

In effect, Washington and his successors implemented the three principles of classical strategy: unity of effort, freedom of action, and strategic proportionality. Further, throughout that formative period, it was understood that domestic strength, assured by the national bank, was our strategic foundation. This lasted until President Andrew Jackson, virulently anti-debt, paid off the national debt, closed the national bank, and plunged the country into depression.

Our greatest Commander in Chief, President Abraham Lincoln, was a self-taught strategist but had what some of us call strategic DNA. After Fort Sumter, SC, was fired upon, Lincoln seized the telegraphs and railways and mobilized the resources of the Nation. As a candidate, he had been anti-slavery; as President, he pivoted, stressing survival of the Republic to keep northern Democrats and border states loyal to the Union. When Lincoln found his generals unwilling to engage Robert E. Lee, he retreated to the Library of Congress to study the classics of strategy and military campaigns. He became his own Grand Strategist. He held tightly to the principles of unity of effort and freedom of action, defying his Cabinet in 1862 by refusing to fight Great Britain over treachery on the high seas. He then executed another strategic pivot, capitalizing on victory at Antietam, MD, to announce the Emancipation Proclamation. This upset the equilibrium of the Confederacy by undermining its alliance with Great Britain.

Lincoln understood that strategic success requires a long view and must be rooted in strategic strength. Even in the middle of our greatest war, Lincoln paid attention to economic and technological growth, investing in a national railroad, creating what has become the national academies, establishing land-grant colleges, and launching the Homestead Act. Finally, he understood a national strategy had to be a **public** strategy. With a command of the language perhaps like none since Shakespeare, Lincoln embraced the role of Persuader in Chief.

Decades after Lincoln's assassination, a Navy Captain at the Naval War College, mocked by his superiors as a mere "pen and ink sailor," drafted the first consciously conceived grand strategy for the United

States. With his book, *The Influence of Sea Power Upon History*, Alfred T. Mahan won acolytes such as Elihu Root, Henry Cabot Lodge, and Theodore Roosevelt for his vision of America as an ascendant world power. I recently delivered an address on Mahan to the U.S. Naval Academy Class of 2012. In his introduction to the printed version, then Chairman of the Joint Chiefs of Staff Mullen noted that the Mahan reform movement was vigorously opposed by senior admirals, but because of his followers, it ended up shaping America's role in the 20th century.

Pursuing Mahan's concepts, Theodore Roosevelt crafted the first global grand strategy by engaging in the Pacific, starting the Panama Canal, increasing international trade, and building a world-class navy backed by a network of bases. Domestically, he engaged the government as a constructive element in our modern economy. Together, these strengths made the United States an agile power and allowed the American Expeditionary Forces to play the decisive role in World War I. The lesson for this conference is that ideas have consequences. Powerful ideas that attract acolytes can move a President and the Nation.

President Franklin Roosevelt read Mahan when he was a teenager and then, when serving as Assistant Secretary of the Navy, helped apply those theories. In 1938, Roosevelt became alarmed about Hitler and executed a strategic pivot as dramatic and significant as Lincoln's in 1862. He told his closest advisor, Harry Hopkins, that the threat of Hitler would eventually engulf the still isolationist America and started crafting what became the grand strategy for winning World War II.

Unlike Lincoln, who lost Colonel Robert E. Lee to the Confederacy, Roosevelt got his man, appointing

General George C. Marshall as Army Chief of Staff. To build what he already envisioned as the Arsenal of Democracy, Roosevelt pivoted from his "soak the rich" campaign rhetoric to recruit Republican business leaders who had opposed the New Deal. After receiving a letter from Albert Einstein warning of Hitler's progress on the atomic bomb, Roosevelt asked Dr. Vannevar Bush, the great scientist-engineer, to mobilize science, engineering, and medicine. Then, echoing Lincoln's watershed second inaugural address, Roosevelt laid the foundation of international peace and cooperation with his Four Freedoms, the Bretton Woods system, and the United Nations conference.

Massive armament production, the development of the atomic bomb ahead of Hitler, and an extensive network of international cooperation are but the most obvious results of these initiatives. We also gained decisive edges in land and sea warfare technologies. At the end of the war, the head of the German Navy said it had been defeated by American science. As Vannevar Bush believed would happen, the benefits of these investments extended far beyond military applications, to national growth and prosperity, and across what he characterized as "the endless frontier." Today, we seem to have forgotten the lessons of that experience.

Contrary to many scholars, I do not see President Harry S. Truman as a grand strategist. Truman became an acolyte of George Kennan, but Kennan's vision of "containment" was a strategic concept, not a Mahan-like vision of grand strategy. He offered neither a philosophy of leadership nor operational initiatives, without which even the best ideas have no legs. As Henry Kissinger noted in his recent review of John L. should this be Gaddis's new biography, Kennan knew this and struggled with it throughout his life. The

Truman doctrine, the Marshall plan, and the North Atlantic Treaty Organization (NATO) alliance made containment functional, but they could not compensate for an ambiguous and incomplete strategic vision.

Congress tried to address the matter of strategy in the National Security Act of 1947, creating the National Security Council (NSC) as a venue for integrating military, economic, and political strategy. Truman ignored this effort, rarely convening the council until the invasion of South Korea in June 1950. The Korean conflict itself may be the best example of the consequences of strategic incoherence. In January, 1950, Dean Acheson— otherwise a great Secretary of State— defined America's strategic interest in the Pacific theater in geographic terms instead of as an extension of containment. When he did not include South Korea within the U.S. "defensive perimeter," North Korea miscalculated and invaded South Korea. North Korea was surprised by U.S. intervention and found itself in a far more protracted and destructive war than it had expected.

When Dwight Eisenhower became President, George Marshall advised him to develop a comprehensive, long-term Cold War strategy incorporating the Truman doctrine, the Marshall plan, and NATO. They agreed that Paul Nitze's *NSC 68* concept, which advocated building for a point of maximum danger, could not be the basis of the strategy. It would continue the ups and downs of defense spending and eventually become unsustainable. Eisenhower's response was Project Solarium, a competitive exercise conducted at the National War College, now the National Defense University.

Project Solarium featured three teams pursuing different strategies to explore various policy options. The results led Eisenhower to conclude that sustainable international power requires a strong, sound domestic economy and broad, bipartisan political and public support. Project Solarium became the basis for Eisenhower's "New Look," his strategy for a sustainable approach to winning the Cold War over the "long haul" and what I would call America's most recent true grand strategy.

To execute his New Look strategy, Eisenhower organized his NSC Staff with a separate, dedicated forward-planning group to look over and across the strategic horizon. He also understood the imperative of proportionality. He is the only President to articulate clear criteria for foreign interventions, laying down five prerequisites. These were the basis for his decision not to assist the French at Dien Bien Phu, Vietnam, during the Indo-China crisis of 1954. Not one of Eisenhower's successors has followed either of these examples.

Like George Washington, Eisenhower started with fiscal strength, focusing on debts and deficits as critical to national power and influence. As Eisenhower emphasized budget cuts, he also emphasized investments. His Interstate Highway Act was a masterpiece of investment in both national security (domestic mobility in the event of attack) and interstate commerce. Eisenhower hired a presidential science advisor, created the Defense Advanced Research Projects Agency, and established the President's Foreign Intelligence Advisory Board and the United States Information Agency. He sought to produce innovative breakthroughs to fuel future growth and international competitiveness, as well as bolster national security.

Where Eisenhower fell short was as Persuader in Chief. Never a big fan of the "bully pulpit," Eisenhower was content to let results speak for themselves. Toward the end of his Presidency, he was increasingly viewed as disengaged and out of touch— assessments that eventually, and unfortunately, attached to his otherwise successful grand strategy, undermining its public support.

In strong contrast, John F. Kennedy entered the White House with a sense of urgency, youthfulness, and new energy. With a focus on both domestic economic power and international leadership, and soaring rhetoric that inspired the nation's youth, Kennedy had the hallmarks of a grand strategist. He was betrayed by a combination of hubris and inexperience, abandoning the NSC system and other elements of Eisenhower's strategic infrastructure, suffering the Bay of Pigs debacle, and facing major crises in Berlin, Germany, and Cuba. Still, along with being a brilliant crisis manager, Kennedy was a serious student of history. In the midst of the Cuban Missile Crisis, he ordered his staff to read Barbara Tuchman's *The Guns of August* to better understand the consequences of miscalculation.

Kennedy also recognized the threat of what we now know as asymmetric warfare, countering the Soviet Union's aggressive engagement in the Third World with an unprecedented commitment to special forces, a strategic investment that is still paying dividends. On balance, Kennedy was a shrewd international strategist who, but for his assassination, might have crafted a new American grand strategy. Sadly, his successor ignored these hard-learned lessons. Though a brilliant legislative strategist, Lyndon Johnson squandered his Presidency on a massive conventional war of attrition.

Like Truman, President Richard Nixon is a textbook example of the difference between brilliant strategic vision and innovation and a true national grand strategy. Nixon campaigned on getting our forces out of Southeast Asia and ending the Vietnam War. Henry Kissinger's extraordinary knowledge of narrative history, along with Nixon's diplomatic skills and mastery of the strategic pivot, combined to produce a secret plan to open China, achieve *détente* with Russia, and isolate North Vietnam, forcing peace negotiations. This approach, coupled with "Vietnamization" to reduce the need for U.S. troops, was working by the end of Nixon's first term. Just 2 years later, though, Saigon fell, and South Vietnam collapsed. This was not the result of bad strategic design, but bad Presidential character. Eisenhower was often quoted as saying, "Trust is the coin of the realm." Without trust, a brilliant strategy is worthless.

President Ronald Reagan was not a strategic intellectual like Eisenhower but, like Franklin Roosevelt, could have transformational vision. Transformational leaders sense moments and opportunities when a strategic pivot can change the course of history. Washington pivoted by backing the Constitutional Convention. Lincoln pivoted after Antietam and again with his second inaugural address. Roosevelt pivoted in 1938. At the Geneva Summit, after meeting alone with him for over an hour, Reagan sized up Soviet General Secretary Mikhail Gorbachev as a man in trouble and looking for a way out. Reagan's advisors all thought he was naïve, but this was his strategic pivot. It began the waltz that ended the Cold War—the culmination of Eisenhower's grand strategy. The NATO alliance of democracies prevailed and could rightly claim what ancient Chinese strategist Sun Tzu called perfect victory—winning without ever having to fight.

The follow-up was fully realized as President George H. W. Bush and his Secretary of State James Baker were able to do the almost impossible—incorporate a united Germany into the Alliance. This set the stage for President Bill Clinton, who led the Alliance to embrace its former enemies—the newly democratic nations of Eastern Europe. But without the uniting threat of the Soviet Union, Presidents Bush, Clinton, and George W. Bush each failed to develop a comprehensive post-Cold War strategy. For each of them, as for President Barack Obama today, preoccupation with near-term crises and distractions has precluded successful long-term strategy making.

A NATIONAL GRAND STRATEGY FOR THE RENEWAL OF AMERICAN LEADERSHIP AND POWER

Going into the 2000 Presidential election, there were two attempts to induce the new president to think in terms of a comprehensive national strategy. One was the congressionally-funded Hart-Rudman Commission. The other was a booklet we produced at what was then known as the Center for the Study of the Presidency, *Comprehensive Strategic Reform: Moving From Inherited Cold War Rigidity to Needed Post-Cold War Anticipation and Agility*. Written a year before September 11, 2001 (9/11), this report noted the weak links in domestic security, the stove-piping of the executive branch, and the lack of agile means: early warning, coalition-building, information sharing, and coherent investment strategy. It called for a President's Strategic Advisory Board, including leaders from outside government to help the President look over and across the horizon. It also recommended a new

Project Solarium. After President George W. Bush was elected, Vice President Dick Cheney and Secretary of Defense Donald Rumsfeld took an interest in our report and created a liaison with our office to pursue these initiatives.

Those joint efforts ended after 9/11, but our efforts have continued. Etched in gold on our conference room wall at the renamed Center for the Study of the Presidency and Congress is Mark Twain's famous adage, "History does not repeat itself, but it can rhyme." Our mission is to find the good rhymes in history and apply them to meet the toughest challenges facing our Nation. Four years ago, in *A Call to Greatness*, I challenged our next President to "relearn the art of strategy." Our Center built on this in our *Strengthening America's Future Initiative*, calling on President Obama and the new Congress to initiate a new Project Solarium and:

> Develop a ten-year national strategy based on a comprehensive assessment and national purpose to align all elements of government and the allocation of resources.

When President Obama entered office, this country was in the midst of a catastrophic recession, fighting two wars, and facing threats from an increasingly hostile and unstable world. As Eisenhower observed, when immediate problems require a President's complete attention, he cannot look over and beyond the horizon to the strategic frontier. Nonetheless, I believe President Obama may have some of the strategic DNA that defined our best Presidents. He gave an extraordinary speech on the role of commander in chief to the Nobel laureates. Emphasizing that domestic renewal and international power go hand in hand, he has focused on restoring America's strength at home, working to get our economic cylinders firing smoothly once again. In a time of budget cuts, Obama has pushed increased investment in education, science, and innovation as tools of national power. He has quite correctly used the specter of rising foreign powers, even the search for a "Sputnik Moment," to justify this integral foundational element of a national grand strategy. What he has not yet been able to do is put all the pieces together. Devoid of private sector experience, Obama has not harnessed the entrepreneurial capabilities of the private sector to rebuild the economy. He has not overcome poisonously partisan politics. He has not united the Nation around a long-term narrative for the way ahead.

In the midst of another presidential election, in which Obama was re-elected, our Center continued the quest to achieve a good rhyme of Eisenhower. We are leading a national conversation about the need for and key elements of a 10-year consensus-building national strategy. Such a grand strategy would overarch two or maybe three Presidents and would be necessarily and consciously bipartisan. We place special emphasis on the reform of the broken parts of our political process and the rebuilding of our domestic capabilities and global competitiveness—the critical pistons of national power referred to earlier.

In looking ahead to the next presidential term and the task of restoring an America with no peers, it is important to understand the multitude of obstacles that any President will face. As an illustration, let us consider what I believe is the greatest example of multinational grand strategy in history: the alliance of democracies that, for more than 60 years, has kept

World War III at bay and has also created the widest distribution of freedom and greatest improvement in living standards ever seen. NATO was the centerpiece and foundation of this strategy, providing both the organizational muscle and the procedural discipline to stay focused over time and through an ever-evolving environment. At the same time, NATO did not define nor limit the underlying strategic goals or vision. Most dramatically, in a move that led directly to internal strife behind the Iron Curtain and despite the opposition of his foreign policy team, President Gerald Ford stepped beyond NATO and backed the Helsinki accords. The point is that our NATO-based strategy had key elements any U.S. President will be hard-pressed to emulate: the ability to retain popular and political support over extended periods and to adapt and renew itself as circumstances require. As Ambassador to NATO in the 1980s, I named our official residence Truman Hall. It is no small irony that the U.S. President most responsible for the success of this international grand strategy struggled and ultimately failed to create an adequate American grand strategy.

Still, some things are clear. In their recent book, *That Used To Be Us*, Thomas L. Friedman and Michael Mandelbaum start by remembering how our schools, our politics, our economy, and our technology were all the envy of the world. In a recent lecture to Phi Beta Kappa, I reviewed the American era of heroic political leadership when such as General George Washington, Speaker of the House and Senator Henry Clay, and President Abraham Lincoln on the cusp of Reconstruction each led the Nation to higher ground through civility, cooperation, and compromise. Not long ago, it was considered patriotic to put country ahead of person, party, and politics. Today, too many of our leaders would have us believe such qualities are character weaknesses. When Standard & Poors downgrades our national credit rating, in part because of a broken system of government and politics, and when a failed "super committee" represented a last, best effort at avoiding policy chaos, it is time to reform the worn-out system of compartmentalized Washington.

This has been done before, just not recently. Both Presidents Roosevelt overhauled the executive branch while in office. Presidents Truman and Eisenhower each utilized commissions chaired by former President Herbert Hoover to manage further reform. Eventually, nearly 200 recommendations from the Hoover commissions were implemented. Most recently, President Nixon turned to industrialist Roy Ash to lead a similar effort during his first term, but Watergate stopped what would have been a radical and much needed bottom-to-top reorganization of the executive branch.

Congress has also reformed itself. Bipartisan, bicameral efforts produced the Legislative Reorganization Acts of 1946 and 1970, strengthening Congress in the face of the vastly enlarged executive branch. A major achievement of the first act was the creation of the Joint Atomic Energy Committee. This effort overcame parochial jurisdictional battles and equipped Congress to deal directly with the emerging threat of a nuclear-armed Soviet Union. A major challenge today is the threat of cyber warfare: many experts believe a coordinated cyber attack could bring the Nation to a standstill. This similar threat demands a similar response: a joint cyber or joint intelligence committee with broad powers would force a compartmentalized executive branch to coordinate efforts and a decentralized private sector to become more collaborative.

As Persuader in Chief, the President must lead this effort personally. In view of the crises we face in governance, President Obama should pledge to carry out an overall reform of the executive branch in his second term and prepare the way for his successor to do so if this is not accomplished. Not only will a pledge like this push Congress to reform its own organization and structure, it will push the President's Republican opponent to respond in kind and thereby change the terms of political debate. While the details of any specific reform proposal will inevitably be a point of partisan difference, the imperative of systemic reform itself should not be. The one thing both parties agree on is that Washington is not working; reform is the only answer. It is the prerequisite to any meaningful new grand strategy. By setting explicit expectations that this can, will, and must happen soon, regardless of partisan control of the House, Senate, or Presidency, the President can create the environment of civility, cooperation, and compromise that is necessary for it to be able to happen.

CONCLUSIONS

Defense Secretary Leon Panetta properly says that "Our job is not to accept destiny; our job is to create destiny." The role of grand strategy is to shape and control the strategic environment. In the face of a dangerous and out-of-control world, grand strategy is the only way to rise above the noise created by crisis after crisis and achieve the promise of our national narrative.

History shows that national grand strategy for the United States can only succeed when grounded in domestic strength and embraced by the American people. History also shows that this requires direct and active presidential leadership. America faces a historic choice: national renewal or national decline. This President and his successor must commit themselves to developing a public consensus on a grand strategy for national renewal, a 10-year strategy that rises above partisan interests and can be continued and completed by their successor as well, regardless of party affiliation. Only by pursuing such a path can America meet its current challenges and rise to new heights. If our President cannot bridge the partisan divide and forge a public strategy that starts with getting our economic engine firing on all cylinders again, our weakened Nation will be choosing decline by default.

America's strategic leadership in the world is not guaranteed. It is something tenuous and precious, constantly vulnerable. We need presidential leadership, in coordination with Congress, to hone the national traits and skills exemplified by the Founding Fathers and to follow Lincoln's injunction to "think anew and act anew." If we fail to preserve what Lincoln called the "last best hope of earth," history, as he also noted, will not forgive us.

CHAPTER 7

GRAND STRATEGY AND
HUMAN THINKING

Evan M. H. Faber

Special thanks to Sheila Ronis for organizing a great conference and for inviting me to speak, and special thanks to my boss and mentor, Leon Fuerth, who has influenced all of my own ideas, but whose ideas I do not represent as a speaker on this panel.

I have a hypothesis that personality plays an under-considered but crucial role in the way that "grand strategy" is viewed as a concept and how it is produced and used in practice. This hypothesis is based particularly on work being done at the Institute for Alternative Futures, an organization that takes a psychology and values-based approach to thinking about the future. They use the Myers-Briggs Type Indicator (MBTI), a model that—while not at all perfect—is useful for assessing personal learning style and preference. For example, of the MBTI types, iNtuitive-Perceiving (N-P) preferences are often paired, as are Sensing-Judging (S-J) preferences.

- N-P types are generally more comfortable with uncertainty and surprise as permanent features of the world. They are generally less comfortable handling measured data and more interested in the big picture that emerges from it. N-P types think more naturally, think in terms of systems, and probably prefer better question-asking to finding concrete answers.
- S-J types, rather, are generally most comfortable with what can be measured and prefer to focus on "the thing itself." Concerned with solving

the problem at hand, S-J types are likely to see the future more or less as a linear extrapolation of the present, with less interest in questioning assumptions and more interest in what is knowable and doable.

This contrast is obviously very general: it certainly does not apply uniformly, there are blends of these kinds of preferences, and this is not a judgment about which way of thinking is better. This is an observation about preference, style of thinking, and people's comfort with different types of analysis. I would venture to guess that the majority of people in this audience fall closer to the N-P type. I would also guess that many of the people that rise to the ranks of top leadership are closer to S-J types, and they rise because of their natural talent for high performance at the tactical and operational level, where N-P types are less likely to distinguish themselves. That means that the people responsible for grand strategy are people whose style is detail focused and evidence oriented. Consequently, having risen to a position where systems-thinking is needed, senior leaders are likely to default to thinking tactically, since they are not innately comfortable thinking in terms of uncertainty, surprise, adaptation, and complex systems in general. That does not mean they are not able; it means it does not come naturally.

Grand strategy demands foresight, which Fuerth defines as the disciplined analysis of alternative futures (and I would add, of hypothetical future contingencies). That means our calling for an American grand strategy is essentially expecting people who are not naturally inclined to think strategically about hypotheticals to make it their regular practice, at a point in their career where their honed style has served them very well. Therefore, for those of us here who believe the United States does not have but needs grand strategy: we need to be able to articulate the case for this kind of thinking to people who are not naturally wired with the instincts of a grand strategist. Not everyone who thinks innately like a grand strategist can rise to the level of a grand strategist, and we cannot sit in the ivory tower yelling that we need grand strategy to people who do not innately operate in this way of thinking. Again, that is not a value judgment, it is an observation about human personality backed up by research.

We need to find new creative ways of communicating the need and the utility of foresight and strategy to those who are concerned with the day-to-day events. New media and advanced information technology (IT) is important for this. Jerry Glenn– another mentor of mine — spoke earlier in the conference about collective intelligence. The ability to link brains, electronic systems, and software to achieve collective intelligence is doable with the technology we have today, and it should be a priority. Instead of watching and reacting as technology evolves, we should actively be shaping it for strategic utility: not just for making our lives more comfortable and convenient, but to make knowledge more useful to decisionmakers. Advanced IT for collective intelligence has the potential to democratize participation in the development of grand strategy by enabling us to organize and harmonize information and perspectives; improve our capacity for disciplined foresight and planning, as well as feedback for learning from results; and therefore also to enhance our ability as individuals and collectives to behave strategically toward achieving goals. The form that technology takes will determine our strategic capacities. We should be guiding development of these tools to expand organizational bandwidth, improve decisionmaking, and visualize complexity for all types of learners and operators.

Enhancing our government organizations means not just incorporating a long view, but a lateral view to watch what is developing and to gauge the approaching impact; to synchronize timing, synchronize investments, and continuously consider implications of oncoming events. There is so much happening at once, and the bandwidth of our organizations is too narrow. We need tools that expand the capacities of our organizations to be able to act intelligently and strategically, and to organize effectively. That is the difference between "strategy" and what Fuerth calls "strategic behavior." If national grand strategy is a top-level activity, then the job of civil society and government bureaucrats cannot be to lock-step march in support of a grand strategy. Strategy needs continuous, active participation. It needs to be taking place in the minds of the people who will execute it at all levels. It is shocking that the people who design strategy for our government are disconnected from the people who run budgets and control the funding streams, all of whom are disconnected from those who implement the strategy. Everyone needs to be involved in the creative process of grand strategy. We are human. When our ego is not engaged, we turn passive. To this end, a "strategic narrative" as proposed by "Mr. Y" is useful as scaffolding around which to synchronize strategic behavior.

I'll close with a comment on "grand strategy." It is possible that the idea of "grand strategy" is actually incompatible with complexity, uncertainty, and surprise. Grand strategy connotes something "static," the production of a large document by a group of people charged with strategy. Suppose you do a large 2-year grand strategy exercise and complete it in, say, December 2010. "Here is our view of the world and our grand strategy," and there it is for everyone to reference. Then in January 2011, you have the Arab Spring, which changes everything. What are you supposed to do? Are you supposed to chuck the whole thing and commence a brand new 2-year grand strategy exercise? That seems like wasted effort, especially in a world where surprise will be the norm for the foreseeable future (meaning more wild cards like the Arab Spring). The point is that "uncertainty" and "complexity" have profound implications for what grand strategy is in **form,** not just substance. Grand strategy itself needs to be dynamic. It needs to be comprised of the requisite variety of potential events and adaptations in its form — literally its **format** — not just in its substance. We have tools for this kind of format — perhaps like a wiki or a Web page. Grand strategy needs to be **used** every day rather than published in a book that gets put on a shelf and occasionally referenced or largely ignored. You cannot produce dynamic strategy using a static strategic document, and we do not have to.

CHAPTER 8

DESIGNING THE U.S. PRESIDENT'S ABILITY TO MAKE STRATEGY

Dr. Robert B. Polk

The year is 2018, and the National Well-Being Act passed by Congress 6 years earlier has already established the new National Planning and Execution Management System. On this day, U.S. President Jennifer Landon prepares for counsel on a brewing international situation. The crisis centers around the country of Pacifica. From President Landon:

> I entered the Think Room of the National Assessment, Visioning, and Integration Center (NAVIC) with my accompanying National Security Staff (NSS) staff and Cabinet leaders. We settled in for the deliberation *experience* orchestrated by the White House Chief of Staff [CofS]. The NAVIC had its work cut out for it. By the end of the 90-minute session, the NSS staff, key Cabinet members, and assisting NAVIC professionals would present all the essential fused aspects of the environment affecting Pacifica. Here I would learn the potential for success or failure.
>
> We used the now venerated *ends, ways, means, thinking, and doing framework* enshrined in *National Planning and Execution Pub 1, version 2.0* to communicate our thoughts. To be clear, the situation in Pacifica was only one of 85 high priority issue areas managed by the NAVIC across the five geographical knowledge bins of this framework. These included the dimensions of space, the globe, regions, countries, and the United States. I was intimately familiar with this framework, as the reports I received daily from the White House CofS and my Cabinet were always broken down into

these same categories. If an issue transcended geographical dimensions, we simply binned them in the next higher concentric frame to track.

Consequently, as I sat in my "captain's chair," I could ask very penetrating questions about Pacifica upon the briefing's conclusion. Because my staff integrated the resource management arm of my executive branch with congressional oversight councils through the NAVIC, I could get a strong sense of what I had at my disposal to affect the Pacifica situation.

The NAVIC's risk assessment and gaming of the NSS preliminary recommendations on Pacifica gave me a good feel for the complexities and potential trade-offs. The NAVIC displayed all this visually, while beaming the conversation in real-time to participants around the country in 3-D with surround sound quality.

I recognized the impact of my options clearly from the presentation *experience* led by the Visioning Team. After my staff and I took our multisensory headsets off, we clearly understood in the most visceral, four-dimensional way that U.S presence on the ground in Pacifica would change lives.

This story offers only a glimpse into a system prototype for strategy making described in my book, *The Thinking and Doing of National Security — A Proposal for the President*. Yet, prototypes are — by definition — unfinished. With collaboration, other solutions will emerge.

Before we arrive at the details of my proposal, I would like to present a select group of expert thoughts that relate to our eventual destination. These include ideas on grand strategy from Professor Russell L. Meade; research related to the human brain as reported by Rebecca Costa in her new book, *The Watchman's*

Rattle; and, finally, the work of authors J. Liedtka and T. Ogilvie on design thinking.

MEADE

My focus on the mechanisms of strategy making seems rather prudent if you join in Meade's assertion that we already have a U.S. grand strategy that works. He describes several components of what he calls America's existing "strategy to dominate the world." First, the United States has established and maintained an open society at home where everyone is welcome, especially his or her ideas. Second, the United States took, "the show on the road" and aggressively engaged with the rest of the world. Third, with its new friends, the United States bought, traded, and grew rich. Fourth, the United States has developed and maintained a geopolitical strategy and vision to match this open economic vision (Meade, 2009).

According to Meade, this global geopolitical strategy ushered in our now default balance of power paradigm. This contributed to a self-beneficial world order where all societies are open to engage and trade with the United States and each other. Such a world order is one in which all global participants could get rich and happy as long as everyone played by the same rules. The hope is and remains that intertwined interests reduce the will for conflict.

According to Meade, the United States rejected the Lighthouse State, where the Bismarck-like figure stands on his pillar and thinks great thoughts in a complicated game of chess with other great figures in other lands. Instead, we evolved into a Mirror State, where the political process reflects the various different voices, coalitions, and interests on board that combine to vector the ship of state. There are no divine thinkers sitting in tall towers. Rather, the state and its people look at history and the patterns of its actions to put various corrective pressures on the system over time. The summation of these vectors determines our destiny.

At the very least, Meade correctly points out that we simply do not keep the ship of state intact long enough to **make** really grand strategy of generational significance. Instead, we are joined on a ship that lurches from side to side, never quite going where we want it to for very long (Meade, 2009) and . . . it has not run aground, yet. I think our future President Jennifer Landon would likely agree with this overall characterization even as she began to explore new ways of evolving her strategies in 2018.

COSTA

Costa, in her 2010 book, *The Watchman's Rattle*, adds color to this conversation. She suggests that our greatest problems are not political; they are biological. Specifically, she reports that science and anthropology converge to prove that the human brain has not evolved to keep up with human progress. Complexity has outpaced the brain's ability to process it. This causes it to hit what she terms a cognitive threshold, defined as the difference between the slow speed at which the human brain can evolve and the rapid rate at which complexity grows (Costa, 2010, p. 188). She argues that all fallen human civilizations suffered in part from this very phenomenon.

Costa answers the so-what of her research by contending that, when societies reach a collective cognitive threshold, they begin a natural coping process.

When individual humans no longer have the time or ability to ascertain facts, they begin to substitute what they know with beliefs. Unchallenged, this can lead to the creation of false memes (beliefs passed unsubstantiated to the next generation) encouraged by false prophets. Some memes grow into super memes and affect the very fabric of whole societies.

Costa goes on to report that the United States is entering such a societal cognitive threshold. Who can argue that the U.S. Congress is not overwhelmed with complexity? How can a single U.S. President fact-check the myriad of important elements in his/her decisionmaking? Who among us understands how the global economy works and what to do about it when it does not? Does anyone have a handle on the intersection of religion and politics anymore? These are just a few opportunities where unsubstantiated beliefs can easily creep into the conversation and create nonevidenced base norms.

Costa argues that the following **super** memes are tearing at the fabric of America today: 1) Irrational opposition to each other and to evidence-based argument. 2) The personalization of blame as the scapegoat for compromise. 3) Counterfeit correlations where causation is no longer the standard. Simple correlation, however falsely conceived, suffices. 4) Silo thinking, where we find it too difficult to see the world as complex and intertwined, leading to solutions that often fall far short of being holistic. 5) Extreme economics where short-term profit is the moral equivalent of the doing what is right even if the long-term negative consequences may be obvious (Costa, 2010, p. 175). These super memes, if they do exist, can cloud or even block any strategic approaches to thinking and doing.

Costa gives hope when she reports how there may be some approaches that can help us break away and move beyond this cognitive threshold. Most importantly, she suggests the increased and deliberate use of insight as a product of left and right brain synthesis. She offers evidence from scientific research on the frontal cortex that supports an emerging ability to call up insight on demand. Here, Costa champions Dr. Michael Merzenich's research on brain fitness, where even simple warm up exercises in the brain can measurably lead to such insight (Merzenich, n.d.).

As a short aside for those of us who call ourselves thinkers, Costa also reports that when viewing brain activity on a computer screen, short-term thinking in humans causes the display to light up like a Christmas tree. However, when given tasks of a long-term nature, that same human brain barely generates a glimmer! Controlled for other variables, the implication is that the brain has not been rewarded by evolution for long-term thinking. Is it any wonder, then, that making strategy is hard? Costa asserts that some evidence even suggests that our brain actively tries to suppress long-term thinking, in evolutionary terms, as superfluous and even harmful to our basic survival needs.

As if the challenge to long-term thinking could not get worse, Costa also notes that:

> When business principles prevail, there is enormous pressure for individuals to respond to complex problems with great speed and efficiency. Quick, decisive action is prized over slower, thoughtful methodical examination. . . .

But then she adds:

> Never mind that [our] leaders possess the same biolog-
> ical apparatus we do and, therefore, are overwhelmed
> by complexity in the same way we are in our daily
> lives (Costa, 2010, p. 172).

Isn't it time we take a closer look at the biological aspects of our human capacity in making strategy?

In the storyline I offered earlier, President Landon understood these limitations all too well and in recognition of this, she immersed herself in the **deliberation experience** to gain advantages over such natural limitations in decisionmaking not available to past leaders. She praised and embraced the new tools that enhance her understanding and improve her participation in strategy making. Finally, she inspired others to do the same.

Costa concludes with a final note on how she would mitigate against these biological limitations and long-held super memes. Reminding us that complexity theory states that there are more wrong solutions than right ones, she suggests that the only way to get at these fewer right solutions is by doing something — anything. Some might say in more technical terms, prototyping using **high failure rate modeling**. The global design thinking community espouses the same and picks up where Costa leaves off.

LIEDTKA AND OGILVIE

According to some, design thinkers are unique in their ability to produce novel and unexpected solutions. They appear to tolerate uncertainty, work with incomplete information, and apply imagination to practical problems using drawings and other modeling media as means to problem solving ("Art of Design_v2.pdf," n.d.). In their book, *Designing for Growth*, Liedtka and Ogilvie support this discussion by offering a testimony from a design-thinking veteran that there are two types of problems — mysteries and puzzles.

Puzzles are problems with an answer. Mysteries are situations where there may not even exist a discernable problem, let alone a solution (Liedtka and Ogilvie, 2011, p. 13). The latter situation is where design thinking distinguishes itself from analysis. It uses visualization, pursues novelty and emotional context, and relies on iterative movement between abstract and practical. It values co-creation with users and prototyping where the object is to learn not launch (Liedtka and Ogilvie, 2011, p. 12).

So why isn't design thinking a more popularly employed technique in the U.S. Government today? Well, as my colleague, T. X. Hammes from the National Defense University, reminded me recently, the challenge of design thinking is in how to translate the iterative process of design into the linear processes of bureaucracy. If anyone could answer this question, it would be the team of Liedtka and Ogilvie.

According to Liedtka and Ogilvie, design thinking can be made practical by applying the following approaches. First, one should explore current reality and frame the challenge (or determining **What is**). Second, one should generate new possibilities for growth (or determining **What if**). Third, one should test assumptions, refine and prototype the concept (or determining **What wows**). Finally, one should enroll customers to shape it into something we can execute (or determining **What works**). There are a number of sub-steps and techniques embedded in each of these but not discussed here (Liedtka and Ogilvie, 2011, p. 21).

None of this is foolproof, of course, and Liedtka and Ogilvie point out that failure to achieve results from design thinking does happen. When it happens, it usually revolves around an inability to connect the concept to an unmet need. Leaders fail to get the results prioritized amid the sea of ideas and priorities. They fail to prototype or visualize the results so others understand it, and they fail to get live customers involved in shaping the results from the beginning (Liedtka and Ogilvie, 2011, p. 178).

One of the most profound aspects of design thinking is its ability "to bypass the culture of debate and help managers learn through action in the marketplace." (Liedtka and Ogilvie, 2011, p. 167) Most of us would also intuitively agree with Liedtka and Ogilvie's claim that:

> . . . the greatest barriers to growth . . . [are an] organization's internal army of designated doubters exercising their veto power before you even have the chance to try (Liedtka and Ogilvie, 2011, p. 184).

So one way to help ease design thinking into an organization is never to call it design thinking. Just do the work and call it whatever you like and, think small . . . at first. Do not push all the ideas at once.

Finally, Liedtka and Ogilvie provide a great list of attributes for a successful design team. Ask yourself if these attributes would be found in most of today's government staffs and leaders. Design teams should have a diversity of skills. They need to listen. They need to find the appropriate framing and create the corresponding strategy, followed by robust analysis.

They use visualization and storytelling to create and communicate. They should check their egos at the door. Teams should co-locate often in a flexible, collaborative physical space. The team should accept a shared purpose. Finally, a successful design team must have top cover from their bosses (Liedtka and Ogilvie, 2011, p. 187). I do not know about you, but I would like to be a part of such a team, and these are the attributes I would want in a national strategy-making organization.

CONCLUSION

Now I want to suggest my own take on how we could roll all these perspectives into a successful system for the thinking and doing in the U.S. Government. I call my approach the National Planning and Execution Management System. I created it as the backdrop to the day-in-the-life story of President Jennifer Landon. Its components consist of the interaction among the President, his/her NSS, the 50 governors, the U.S. departments, as well as the public at large and the Congress.

My system begins with framing any conversation on strategy making into five concentric bins of knowledge. Any issue that could affect the viability and vitality of the Nation will find a home in one of these bins. These bins are: space, the globe, regions, countries, and internal U.S. matters. This common framework allows all participants to share their narratives about the future in ways that promote fast learning. This also sets the foundation for actionable participation in generating new ideas.

I realize that, at first glance, such a framework seems to defy modern reality that most of our problems today — from global warming to health concerns and the economy — abide by no boundaries. Yet, every transboundary issue imaginable can be binned in one of these categories. Each of these broad categories is further sub-organized into the time frames of near-, mid-, and long-term. The intersections of these time frames and geographical knowledge bins contain the various national strategies for linking the ways and means to all stated ends for every issue and area of concern. This thinking and doing framework would serve as a template across all the participants in the National Planning and Execution Management System.

The linchpin of this system would be a newly established capability called the NAVIC, housed within the Executive Office of the President (EOP). The NAVIC would never make policy but instead provide visioning, assessment, and strategy-making services up to the NSS and Congress. The NAVIC would provide these same services to the governors and the U.S. Cabinet. It would integrate all these services and synthesize the feedback and lessons learned into new approaches for the President and the NSS to consider. Finally, selected congressional entities would have an unprecedented access high and early in the executive processes within the NAVIC. These are just a few of the functions presently conceived.

The NAVIC would serve the NSS as its primary client, and it is from the NSS that the NAVIC would get its priorities. These services would free the already beleaguered NSS to stay focused on its primary duties of advising the President on the national ends (or policy), while leaving the NAVIC and the Cabinet to devise and integrate the ways and means.

The NAVIC would deploy state-of-the-art facilities and cutting edge visual decision support aids. It would provide continuity on matters across the spectrum of national organizations with its common informational connectivity across the breadth of actors. The mirrored capabilities positioned in the 50 states would also provide the President multiple redundant command center capabilities.

The NAVIC would emphasize the integration of both thinking and doing under one roof, supported by a modest staff working for six functional directors confirmed by the Senate. Members would be appointed for 15-year tours reporting to one presidentially appointed Executive Director. The Executive Director would also serve as the deputy to the President's Chief of Staff to ensure the overall system serves at the pleasure of the President.

So this is the system that President Landon inherited to cohere the full breadth and depth of the U.S. Government more effectively in making strategy. She used this to mitigate threats and to take advantage of opportunities that affected the viability and vitality of the Nation in the near-, mid-, and long-term. Her system included the human and organizational dimensions of thinking and doing as equal sides of the same coin. This helped her develop the visions through the human-centered process of design leading to strategy that matched appropriate ways and means to her designated ends.

I want this chapter to serve as a beginning. The ideas and details expressed in my book could be used as a starting prototype. Think of it as throwing the proverbial pasta on the wall to see what sticks. I am quite certain Steve Jobs didn't hand us the iPhone on his first try. Instead, his team must have prototyped dozens, perhaps hundreds, of times before going to a pilot and only then to a launch. Washington is awash in studies and conferences, but these will only carry us so far. My dream is to move our thinking into action through iterative prototyping. We should follow the great design company IDEO's creed to **fail faster to succeed sooner**. I hope this chapter and my book may spark others to take up this challenge.

REFERENCES

ArtofDesign_v2.pdf. (n.d.). Retrieved from *usacac.army.mil/cac2/CGSC/events/sams/ArtofDesign_v2.pdf.*

Costa, R. (2010). *The Watchman's Rattle: Thinking Our Way Out of Extinction* (First Ed., First Printing.). New York: Vanguard Press.

Liedtka, J., & T. Ogilvie. (2011). *Designing for Growth: A Design Thinking Toolkit for Managers.* New York: Columbia University Press.

Merzenich, M. (n.d.). Dr. Michael Merzenich's Brain Fitness Program: "You Can Rejuvenate Your Memory And Your Abilities To Learn" DeansGuide. Retrieved October 27, 2011, from *deansguide.wordpress.com/2007/12/15/dr-michael-merzenichs-brain-fitness-program-you-can-rejuvenate-your-memory-and-your-abilities-to-learn/.*

Polk, R. B. (2010). *The "Thinking and Doing" of National Security: A Proposal for the President.* Bloomington, IN: Trafford Publishing.

Meade, Russell L. (December 10, 2009). U.S. Grand Strategy — from Theory to Practice. *Rethinking Seminar Series.* Retrieved October 27, 2011.

CHAPTER 9

THE NEED FOR GRAND STRATEGY DEVELOPMENT: LESSONS FROM THE PROJECT ON NATIONAL SECURITY REFORM AND SINGAPORE

Dr. Sheila R. Ronis

INTRODUCTION

The Vision Working Group (VWG) of the Project on National Security Reform (PNSR) recommended the establishment of a Center for Strategic Analysis and Assessment (CSAA) in its July 2010 *Report and Scenarios* (Ronis, 2010). Over a 5-year period of study, the PNSR VWG established that the United States needs a place, a process, and a set of capabilities in the Executive Office of the President (EOP) to develop and test grand strategies for the Nation, particularly to support the national security system.

The *National Security Strategy* is the best representation of a comprehensive discussion of where the country is going and what it wants to accomplish. Published by The White House from time to time, it is neither sufficiently long term nor a true strategy that links resources with objectives over time. It represents, at best, a list of aspirational goals by an administration. In a world of increasing complexity, the United States should consider long-term, whole-of-government thinking and planning. Other countries have established such a set of capabilities within the heart of their governments, such as the United Kingdom and Singapore. For that reason, the set of capabilities in Singapore was benchmarked, because the VWG develops specificity for the proposed Center. This document represents a synthesis of lessons learned from the Singapore system, recognizing that not all of the processes are scalable to the U.S. Government.

THE CONTEXT

For decades, the private sector has routinely used management tools such as forecasting, scenario based planning, strategic visioning, political and economic risk assessments, etc., but the government, especially in a whole-of-government way, rarely, if ever, uses such tools across the board, although sometimes those tools are used in pockets — in specific agencies or departments.

The question is, "What mechanisms should the U.S. Government develop to improve the Nation's ability to plan in a whole-of-government way for its future — to be better prepared for a future that is very different from its past?" At the end of World War II, General George C. Marshall said, "We are now concerned with the peace of the entire world, and the peace can only be maintained by the strong." (Marshall, 1945) But, how does the United States remain strong? What does that mean in a world of globalization? How should the country define what national security is in such a complex and interdependent world?

The PNSR VWG took a systems approach to examining this series of questions. The group stepped out into the next larger system, and the system beyond that, to look across the entire mosaic at the elements and their interdependence and interactions to better understand the whole and its behavior. The study engaged in both analysis and synthesis and used visioning tools to assist in testing the creation of the new structures, policies, strategies, and processes necessary for a successful 21st century national security system as outlined in *Forging a New Shield*, (PNSR, 2008) the overall study presented to the President of the United States, The President-elect, and the U.S. Congress in December 2008.

U.S. security is rooted in the successful integration of all major elements of national power: economic, diplomatic, military, informational, and so on. When successfully combined, the vitality of the nation is ensured, and the country's ability to encourage positive change throughout the globe is enhanced. The PNSR proposed a modern apparatus to serve the nation's needs well into the 21st century to support the broad national security challenges and address the interagency mechanisms in the organizational space between the President of the United States and the Cabinet level agencies and departments.

The VWG asked the question, "What is the basis for rethinking the national security system, and how will success in the future be characterized?" If "what is" and "what is not" in the arena of national security is artificially or prematurely narrowed, it is likely that situations will be misread that can ultimately, and negatively, affect the Nation. Ten years ago, the challenges related to sub-prime mortgages, diseased birds, automobile emissions, and pilot training rosters were not typically the focus of national security. Today, it is clear that they might well have been. The point is no one can imagine or determine now with certainty what might affect the Nation in the future.

Threats can be assessed and prioritized based upon considerations such as urgency, impact, magnitude, mitigation options, and intention. Opportunities can be assessed and prioritized based upon considerations such as knowledge, expertise, probability of success, resources, long-term sustainability, proportionality, and intention.

Based on this approach, national security can be considered "Any situation, condition, or entity that has the potential to enhance or degrade the viability and vitality of the nation" (Benner, 2007), so that the national security system would be responsible for and measured by:

- the viability and vitality of the Nation,
- peaceful and positive development throughout the countries of every region, and
- cooperation and collaboration around the globe.

The national security system needs to become a "learning organization" that can anticipate, adapt to, and successfully address the widest range of threats and opportunities for both the good of the Nation and the world. As a complex adaptive system, the future security system will need to possess certain inherent qualities that will be critical to success. It must:

- share information and collaborate horizontally,
- accommodate unanticipated needs and partnerships,
- ensure agility in the face of uncertainty,
- incorporate ad hoc structures and processes, and,
- maintain a long-term view.

Because the U.S. national security system is a complex adaptive system, it is difficult to separate geopolitical, social, and economic phenomena. These elements interact as a system of systems. In fact, in most instances, it is a complex system of complex systems, and that is the challenge facing the Nation.

The environment of the 21st century is, and will continue to be, characterized by rapid change and continuing uncertainty. Many factors contribute to a security landscape that differs greatly from the world envisioned at the end of the Cold War and even more since 9/11. Simply put, globalization has resulted in a world that is increasingly interconnected and interdependent. Readily available technology, environmental degradation, global capital market collapses, transnational terror, global disease, cyber attacks, and a host of other concerns have added complexity to the national security landscape. These volatile, uncertain, and complex ambiguities of the strategic environment, as taught at the U.S. war colleges, will demand the application of a wide range of traditional and innovative strategies and tactics to counter threats and take advantage of opportunities.

Based upon both the realities being faced today and the context emerging for tomorrow, the following are basic observations. First, the world is a system, like a spider web. Movement or damage in one spot has the potential to be felt throughout the entire web. Like in a pond, while the ripples may be visible closest to where the stone is thrown, the entire pond feels some level of movement and/or impact. Global interdependence is now a reality, and national security issues must always assume a global focus.

Second, the nation's homelands are no longer protected by distance or time. The great oceans that buffered the United States from much of the world, for example, no longer serve as boundaries. Therefore, the distinction between foreign affairs and homeland concerns has become blurred — perhaps even nonexistent for all. National security is a merged "mess" of internal, external, and interdependency issues, and this has enormous consequences for dealing with national security issues.

Third, the reality of globalization demands a holistic worldview alongside specific national interests. The needs and concerns of every country must be developed in concert with the welfare and security of the entire globe. To participate in globalization requires new ways of connecting to everyone else on the planet to ensure that all are secure — being a rogue nation, or having rogue citizens, can change everything in ways that are far reaching.

More than 2,400 years ago, ancient Chinese Philosopher Sun Tzu said in his masterpiece, *The Art of War*,

> If you know your enemy and you know yourself, you need not fear the result of a hundred battles.
>
> If you know yourself but not the enemy, for every victory gained, you will suffer a defeat.
>
> But if you know neither yourself nor the enemy, you will succumb in every battle (Tzu, ~400 B.C.).

In today's global context, this quotation suggests that if a nation is in any kind of competition, it must be familiar with, and develop knowledge of, its competitors as well as itself if success is to be expected. How well have nations developed relationships with their partners and friends to ensure cooperation when there is a problem anywhere on the globe? No one is big enough or wealthy enough to truly cover the world in terms of knowledge and/or capabilities.

In a 1957 speech, General Dwight D. Eisenhower said, "Plans are worthless, but planning is everything." (Eisenhower, 1957) President Eisenhower is explaining that through the knowledge learned in planning processes, plans are more likely to be successful. This is learning in the Sun Tzu sense.

The complex systems within the national security community have interesting characteristics worth identifying and discussing. Probably the most important characteristic is that complex systems cannot be controlled — at best, they can be influenced. The systems can only be influenced if understood intimately; what the late American statistician Dr. W. Edwards Deming calls "profound knowledge" of a system (Deming, 2000).

The CSAA needs to be a learning organization to support whatever national security structure is in place in the United States. The Center would be created to learn, analyze, assess, and synthesize risk, foresight, and the development of "grand strategy." Government policymakers may want the Center to predict. But, prediction assumes theories, and theories require assumption testing to learn. The complexity sciences say that, in complex systems, there are limits to what can be learned or known with any precision; you can predict probabilities but not certainties. Even in physics, the Heisenberg Uncertainty Principle says if some things are known, other variables cannot be known. Such is the case in the national security system. Many policymakers expect prediction and control of the real world complex systems they are supporting. In the real world, complexity science is clear. Prediction and control of complex adaptive systems is impossible with certainty.

One of the VWG findings included the need to synthesize "all of government" solutions to complex system issues and problems; and sometimes "all of society." The only successful way to do that is to be learning about the system issues — in hyper learning modes using accelerated learning processes and coupling those with foresight tools such as Delphi techniques. These enable the development of scenarios for planning . . . and ultimately being able to develop "grand strategies." The VWG also found that the United States needs to systematically use these tools and processes to improve decisionmaking and create mechanisms for that to happen at the whole-of-government level — at the level of the President.

The CSAA in the EOP will develop scenarios and "grand strategies" to apply lessons learned in a world of complexities, and that requires context and synthesis. It also requires breaking down the stovepipes of government so they can work together effectively. Mechanisms to use complex systems thinking and foresight tools in the decisionmaking processes of the executive branch of the government need to be developed.

PNSR VWG Scenario Development Process.

To begin the process, the PNSR VWG began by asking the question, "How can foresight be used to have an impact on presidential decisionmaking in the context of the uncertainties inherent in an interconnected, fast-changing world?" (Ronis, 2010) The findings of the overall PNSR effort were stress tested by developing a set of scenarios to see if they improved system performance. In addition to complementing and enhancing the overall PNSR findings, the visioning process resulted in detailed scenarios against which specific options generated by the Project were assessed.

The process used to develop the scenarios began by determining the purpose and scope of the scenarios. Since The National Security Act of 1947 survived largely intact for more than 60 years despite major social, technological, economic, environmental, and political changes, the VWG looked ahead about 50 years. The Nation will face extraordinary changes during this time. Most forecasters and technologists believe that the rate of change in the next decades will accelerate so rapidly that it will be difficult to imagine.

It was with this in mind that the VWG created scenarios that would provoke discussion and debate within the Project and hopefully lead to better, more resilient recommendations. The next step required the development of a questionnaire to be given to experts representing some of the best minds in the Nation. For that process, experts in many fields, including a cross section of the sciences and engineering, in particular the national academies, were enlisted. The best approaches to the development of a survey instrument were examined, and a questionnaire was developed to solicit the input of experts in many fields. The national academies hosted a conference to explore these issues, and, based on the findings, the survey instrument was finalized.

The VWG then created a list of experts to receive the questionnaire in many disciplines across the sciences, engineering, arts, futurists, and other fields too numerous to mention. The experts' viewpoints would be critical to the successful development of scenarios that would be based on their projections of the future.

The questionnaire was then sent to over 1,500 experts who were queried via email about the future of their disciplines. It was hoped that 2-3 percent would return their opinions regarding the future to ensure a sufficient population. The Project obtained 133 responses, a 9 percent response, and the responses represented a full spectrum of disciplines. The experts' insights on future trends and milestones were aggregated, analyzed, and synthesized to better understand the ways that the future could unfold. The trends identified by the experts were then woven into nine scenarios representing three time horizons—2020, 2040, and 2060.

Before the scenarios could be used to stress test the recommendations of the Project, the VWG asked the commandants of three major schools at the National Defense University to choose selected faculty who taught in the national security curriculum of each school to read all nine scenarios and give the VWG feedback regarding the scenarios. The scenarios were then stress tested with the national security faculty at the National War College, the Industrial College of the Armed Forces, and the Joint Forces Staff College. Based on the feedback of the faculty, adjustments were made.

The five major solution sets of the Project were then stress tested by the Working Group Leaders, using all nine scenarios developed. As a caveat, the scenarios were intentionally designed to stress the working group's recommendations from several angles. The scenarios should not be viewed as predictions, but rather glimpses into plausible alternative futures. The scenarios are intentionally inconsistent and oft times bleak, all in the interest of provoking a wider range of conversation.

For each scenario, five general questions were used in testing the solution sets.

1. What are the stressors in the scenario?

2. How well was the system able to anticipate the scenario problems?

3. If the system was not able to prevent/remove the threat, how well was the system able to react?

4. How well was the system able to recover?

5. How well does the system function as a whole—specifically, the structures and processes?

As the working group leaders worked through the scenarios, it was clear that each solution set performed differently in the different scenarios. Strengths and weaknesses of the solution sets gradually emerged.

Each scenario is followed by specific discussion questions to ponder.

1. How will the recommendations function in the scenario presented?

2. Are there problems or solutions identified that have not been addressed?

3. If this future is not desirable, what choices should be made today to avoid it?

The 2020 scenarios include:

Scenario 1: Red Death, in which the country is struggling to get back on its feet after a major biological attack and witness a debate about the future role of the U.S. Government both at home and abroad. Half of the world's population perishes in this disturbing scenario.

Scenario 2: The People's War, in which the United States faces global asymmetric warfare against a nuclear-armed great power. The entire federal government is caught in the conundrum of how to respond to anonymous attacks at home and abroad, while avoiding an escalation to nuclear war.

Scenario 3: A Grand Strategy, in which the utility of an integrated grand strategy development capability is explored for smoothing the transition from one presidential administration to another, the time when the country is most vulnerable.

The 2040 scenarios include:

Scenario 4: A New Economy, in which the United States faces its worst economic crisis since the Great Depression. The crisis is a perfect storm of the unintended consequences of new technologies, policies, court decisions, and popular expectations.

Scenario 5: Army of One, in which the intersection of unmanned, robotic warfare and, on the ground, assisted diplomacy, is explored. This scenario depends upon the continuation of current trends in robotics and sensors technology, as well as a public policy choice to enable greater real-time interaction between the military and diplomatic arms of the U.S. Government.

Scenario 6: Who Holds the High Ground, in which major competitive changes in the Earth-Moon system are envisioned from the perspective of a traditional interagency space working group.

Scenario 7: A Brave New World, in which a plan is examined to apply proven neuroscience, psychiatric, and medical techniques to control pathological behaviors in a world of readily accessible weapons of mass destruction and genetic engineering.

The 2060 scenarios include:

Scenario 8: A Warm Reception, in which the challenge of developing international consensus for action on the issue of global climate change and the possibility of unintended consequences is focused.

Scenario 9: It is a Small World, in which the implications of a very different future are explored, wherein small, molecular scale machines (nanotechnology robots or "nanobots") have become ubiquitous.

Finally, the possibility of a technological singularity by 2060 is noted, when robots will be smarter than human beings and the unknown effects of life on earth.

The scenarios demonstrated that the five major findings of the PNSR significantly improved system performance.

Singapore Examples for Benchmarking.

By studying the Strategic Policy Office, National Security Coordination Secretariat, National Security Coordination Centre, Horizon Scanning Centre, Centre for Strategic Futures and the Risk Assessment, and Horizon Scanning Centre in the Office of the Prime Minister and the Centre of Excellence in National Security at the S. Rajaratnam School of International Studies at Nanyang Technological University, there are many lessons that will assist in the establishment of the U.S. Center.

According to Peter Ho of the Singapore Civil Service, there are four major roles for their Centre for Strategic Futures, all of which should be represented in the U.S. EOP Center's set of capabilities (Ho, 2010). These roles are:

- "Challenge conformist thinking" by building global networks and partnerships with academia, think tanks, and global thought leaders through conferences and projects;
- "Identify emergent risks" by creating risk maps and communicating emerging issues to decisionmakers;
- "Calibrate strategic thinking processes" by using scenario planning and risk assessment to develop policy and new capabilities; and,

- "Cultivate capabilities, instincts, and habits," by using systems and strategic frameworks and mindsets to deal with uncertainty, disruptive shocks, and whole-of-government approaches regularly.

This set of capabilities and mindsets represent a strategic capability for Singapore that, although not specifically scalable to the United States, would certainly enhance the capabilities within the EOP, if adopted in the United States.

The Center for Strategic Analysis and Assessment.

The scenarios used in the PNSR study represent the kind of creative systems thinking that the United States needs today—the kind of thinking that should be infused in the CSAA. The Nation needs to support strategic decisionmaking in an interagency whole-of-government manner at the highest levels for issues of national importance and/or security.

This can be accomplished by the establishment of the Center, which will be a place, a process, and a set of capabilities that enable the development and use of forward-looking global contexts improving decisions by integrating all major elements of national power—economic, diplomatic, informational, defense, and others—to assess second, third, and fourth order effects of decisions and develop "grand strategy" where necessary. Singapore represents an example of where this kind of thinking is thriving.

The Center should provide a rigorous framework to analyze, synthesize, test assumptions, develop red team solution sets, and integrate the elements of national power to provide contexts to support long-term strategic decisions. The Center will support the integration of the nation's near-, mid-, and long-term national security planning based on pragmatic internal (U.S.) and external (the world) assessments and aspirational visions of what the future could be. The center would endeavor to help translate policies made by the various EOP offices into plans for the interagency space.

The Center should provide comprehensive exercises to support the development of grand strategies and policies in the interagency. It should continually develop scenarios, table-top "games," and simulations, anticipating areas that should be strategically thought about to inform policy and strategy development.

Networking and Outreach.

The Center should provide workshops and seminars as well as outreach activities to the private sector, academia, think tanks, communities of practice, and the American people. It should provide long-term planning capabilities to maintain unity of purpose over successive administrations and generations of leadership. For all the things the CSAA will do, it should not develop policy. It should *inform* the development of policies and grand strategies by providing context and testing assumptions of those making policy and strategy decisions.

Annually, The CSAA should host a "State of the World" conference in which its members will share lessons learned from the systems, processes, and scenarios developed in the Center. Internal staff promotions and cross-training among experts will be critical to inform future national policy and strategy leadership with fused, strategic thinking capabilities.

One role of the Center should be to ensure that strategic American and global assets—human, material and those related to our national power—are known and employed strategically and systematically when needed. The Center will need to operate in both open and classified environments, depending on the needs of the President and the issue being discussed or studied.

Examples of scenarios that might be developed in the Center should include:

- U.S. energy independence solution sets,
- Global religious extremism issues and strategies,
- Strategies to improve science, technology, engineering, and mathematics graduate degrees by U.S. citizens,
- Increasing U.S. children's science and mathematics scores for 6th, 9th, and 12th grades,
- Universal health care sustainability,
- Industrial base incentives,
- Palestinian-Israeli peace talks,
- Wargaming, and
- Peace gaming and everything in between.

Grand strategy assessments of major recommended policy initiatives should be cross-walked with an interagency mindset across all elements of national power.

There are two strategic weaknesses of the United States that regularly keep the Nation from looking at its future in a strategic and systemic way and preparing itself for that future. The United States does not engage in strategic visioning or foresight exercises, and it does not write and/or execute grand strategies

as a nation. It needs to do both. Worst of all, it does not even think this way.

The Center should be established within the interagency and continuously develop scenarios of the future. This will help senior government policymakers plan for an integrated future across the entire government spectrum, including the Congress. This will probably include congressional committee reform that creates interagency mission funding mechanisms through intercommittee decisionmaking processes across jurisdictional boundaries. Systems thinking provides the framework that establishes the need to break down the barriers in the stovepipes of government from the top to the bottom.

Finally, within the Center, the Nation needs to help senior government policymakers plan for the role the United States will play in that future, including how the United States will remain strong in the Marshall sense. Although originally conceived to "fit" into other national security reforms, the capabilities of the Center need to be established within the EOP with or without the other reforms envisioned (PNSR, 2008).

Assessment Capability.

The Assessment Center's capability should be developed using the five essential planning perspectives of 1) space, 2) the planet, 3) regions, 4) countries, and 5) U.S. internal (domestic) for each of the three time cycles of near-, mid-, and long-term. Each of these near-, mid-, and long-term assessments would include both geographic and functional dimensions.

The assessment of risk needs to encompass system risk most of the time. Frequently, the impact of a particular course of action has an economic or political risk associated with it. But, risk in a world of complexity requires an understanding not only of individual risk variables, but also of the interactions of risks associated with all of the system variables across the spectrum from sociological, technological, economic, environmental and political (STEEP) risk. Frequently, the risk must be accumulated, and the algorithms need to take into consideration the amount of risk and the associated influence of multiple risk factors at the same time. Only when all of the risk is accounted for in a system can a risk variable be calculated. System risk is the aggregation and understanding of the many forms of risk that occur internal and external to the system but which potentially have an impact on the system — the product of the interactions and interdependencies of the various forms of STEEP risk. See Figure 9-1.

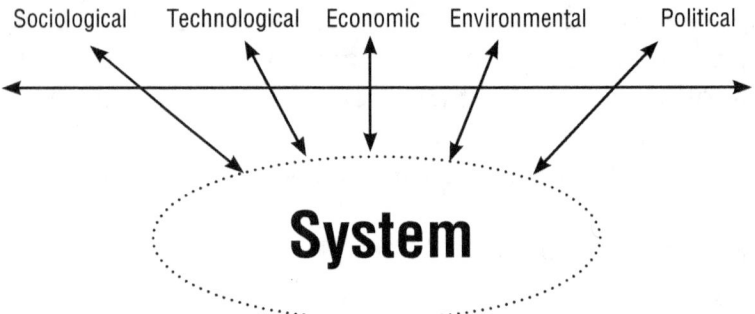

"System Risk" is the aggregation and understanding of the many forms of risk that occur internal and external to the system but which potentially have an impact on the system—the product of the interactions and interdependencies of the various forms of risk, sociological, technological, economic, environmental and political.

Figure 9-1. System Risk across the STEEP Variables.

Visioning Capability.

Visioning would produce both pragmatic and "what-if" scenarios to test assumptions, ends, ways, and means of plans. The Center will include various inputs from the U.S. intelligence community, homeland security, private industry, and international entities as needed.

The Center should provide the President with an ability to immediately take stock of the status of both the internal system and the external environment, as well as to understand the decision points necessary to maintain his/her policy objectives in the near-, mid-, and long-term across the whole of government in the five planning perspectives. The Center director would be a senate confirmed member of the EOP at an executive level, and the staff would be comprised of a majority of full-time civil servants to provide continuity between administrations. Consequently, the director should have rank commensurate to this responsibility. This position should be Senate-confirmed for two reasons: 1) to help satisfy the desire for congressional oversight over this most central function of the executive branch; and 2) to help this official garner the support of the wider interagency in this process. This person should therefore be at the rank equivalent to the President's highest directors in the EOP, just one position in rank below the National Security Advisor or Chief of Staff. The Center Director should brief the President formally once a month but would sit on any EOP committees as required.

Advisors and contractors from outside of government would likely be a part of the Center in the preparation of its work products since the Center expects to keep some of its hires as part-timers, and this might include work done by contracted advisors from outside government in order to keep the Center on the highest edges of evolving technologies and processes for its mission accomplishment.

The President of the United States should have a place and a process to conduct grand strategy on issues of national importance and security. The Center, within the EOP, should develop and support many functions and capabilities in support of the development of these grand strategies.

The Gaming Function.

One of the most critical functions of the Center should be the capability for gaming issues of national importance and security in support of the development of grand strategy. Gaming is usually considered the process of thinking through events in a step-by-step, point and counterpoint fashion to explore possible outcomes of certain courses of action over others. These processes enable the use of various exercises to think through potential situations before decisions are made. The processes should be developed to ensure a thorough investigation and analysis of the situation by exploring positions on all sides of the question involved. These capabilities will range from "red teaming" proposed courses of action to developing step-by-step tabletop exercises meant to role play situations in foreign policy or peace negotiations to the development of alternative visions of the future and calculating risks associated with each one to determine which set of decisions should be made and which policies should be implemented to create the preferred future state.

Gaming is a form of scenario based planning. Gaming processes improve the ability to develop strategies and policies or choose specific decisions over others in a world of uncertainty. The objective of a game, however, is not to predict behaviors but to learn about the potential of certain behaviors and their effects over others and to learn which sets of behaviors, and therefore outcomes, might be best for the "end game" you want. Games are structured thinking processes that ultimately produce analysis and synthesis to improve decisionmaking regarding strategies and policies. It requires holistic and systems thinking about issues.

The spectrum of games available in the Center will include traditional scenario based "stories" associated with specific interagency issue or country teams and grand strategy level issues such as "energy independence by 2050" or "sustainable peace in the Middle East." The gaming capabilities within the Center will be available at many different levels of scale and complexity depending on the needs. Levels from grand strategy to tactical concerns are levels of scale. Levels of complexity can also be varied, depending on the sets of issues to be examined. Levels of sophistication can also vary from the use of tabletop exercises that use pencils and paper to the use of algorithms in the development of software that can facilitate a variety of games using simulations in computers.

Games can be developed at any level of system scale. The grand strategy level will be used to describe the highest level of strategy needed, usually at the global or country-to-country level. The strategic level will imply the whole agency or department level or the level of an institution such as the Army. The operational level will imply a lower level of an organization such as a directorate or a battalion level. The tactical level can go as low as the individual in a group or a small group such as a platoon level.

What is most important is that the mission of the exercise be identified so that clear objectives can be written and exercises developed to accomplish the mission. All games should have one thing in common: to facilitate learning about a particular topic, course of action, or policy decision to better understand the dynamics of the environment surrounding the issue, the issue itself, the stakeholders, and players involved. Games are studies. In particular, decisions should be thought through looking holistically at the situation and determining the 2nd, 3rd, and 4th order effects of decisions involved. For example, tools as diverse as causal loop diagramming and mathematical techniques of operations research will be available in the Center and available for gaming as needed. Causal loop diagrams visually "map" the relationships between phenomena and decisions. Operations research techniques are frequently used to study costs and effectiveness of judgments. Many methods for strategy and policy analysis, synthesis, and systems thinking will be used. In fact, all suitable methods within the structured and disciplined processes that will enable better thinking will be used in the Center. According to Richard Kugler in his seminal work *Policy Analysis in National Security Affairs: New Methods for a New Era:*

> . . . the U.S. Government will continue to face many difficult decisions in the national security arena because the future is hard to see, and the consequences of alternative policies are hard to predict . . . systems analysis can help improve the quality of these decisions . . . it can help the Government think clearly in times of uncertainty and during noisy debates about policy and strategy (Kugler, 2006).

Most of the games employed in the Center will be developed for the Center but will draw upon the myriad games that have been used over decades to think through "war" scenarios but with other themes, including economic, diplomatic, and environmental issues and the traditional war-peace issues that games have played in the past. Learning through play is a major way to prepare for the future, not only for children, but also for all who need to use imagination and knowledge, coupled with experimentation, to practice the way forward—using games. As Arie De Gues says in *The Living Company: Habits for Survival in a Turbulent Business Environment*, when describing the original Royal Dutch Shell scenario process development:

> . . . the decision-making process is in fact a learning process in any company and there are ways to improve the speed, if not the quality, of the decisions. The more in depth the simulation, and the more that 'play' triggers the imagination and learning, the more effective the decision-making process seems to be. In companies that attempt large-scale internal change, this is particularly true. Decisions cannot be made in the old authoritarian manner. They need interaction, intuitive reflection, and the fostering of collaborative mental models. They need play. They need learning (De Gues, 1997).

New gaming and analytical tools need to be honed in The Strategy Center. They will continuously improve over time. As Robert Lempert argues in Francis Fukuyama's *Blindside:*

> Policy-makers may not always welcome a critical spotlight on the potential weaknesses of their proposed strategies. But, if rigorous assessment of sur-

prise becomes as commonplace as budgeting and accounting, policymakers will find it harder to ignore (Fukuyama, 2007).

The Center will further make use of these assessments to engage in medium- and long-term projections of future threats, risks, and opportunities, again incorporating diverse and interrelated elements such as economic, diplomatic, societal, environmental, technological, military, and so forth.

The Center can be tasked by any agency, or by the President, to assess, game out, or develop grand strategies for problems in which impacts and solutions cut across multiple government agencies. Such assessments and solution sets will be presented to each affected agency to provide a basis for cooperation, policy formulation, and/or resource allocation.

Engage in Rigorous Problem Analysis.

Effective policies must be grounded in rigorous problem analysis incorporating both a multidisciplinary approach and sensitivity to the ways in which policies will affect other variables. Failing that, policies may be made based on false or outdated assumptions or may produce unintended consequences in the long-term. Currently, the various organizations of the federal government are host to exceptional bodies of knowledge and expertise. Yet the ability to engage in rigorous problem analysis in crafting policies is hindered by a number of factors.

The demands of urgent emerging national challenges, coupled with limited human resources, frequently preclude rigorous problem analysis. This is especially true when doing so requires drawing on diverse competencies spanning multiple agencies or departments.

Nowhere does the capability exist to test thoroughly the assumptions of analysts, which may prove false, outdated, or incomplete. Their conclusions, moreover, are invariably aimed at achieving short-term objectives, and they lack the ability to thoroughly assess the medium- and long-term impacts of proposed policies. Finally, the quality of problem analysis can be hindered by the inevitable loss of institutional memory sustained through turnovers in human resources with successive administrations. The Center should seek to remedy these shortcomings. Unburdened by the need to make or implement policy itself, it is wholly devoted to problem analysis, research, scenario development, gaming, and assessment.

The Center should continuously develop scenarios and provide assessments of the global climate and of emerging national challenges. Decisionmakers can also task the Center to engage in specific projects where the agencies lack the resources to conduct such analysis themselves or where the issues transect multiple departments or agencies. Its research, which employs a variety of analytic and testing tools and draws on a broad range of expertise, will help inform policies and grand strategy in the interagency.

The Center should also provide a rigorous framework to analyze and test assumptions, as it continually develops scenarios, games, and simulations to anticipate the effects and secondary impacts of potential solution sets and proposed policies into the medium and long term. Finally, the Center seeks to facilitate finding, identifying, and storing national and global assets, both human and physical, as needed to develop specific expertise.

Facilitate Long-term Planning and Preserve Institutional Memory.

As the rate of change and the complexity of challenges continue to increase, there is little doubt over the value of conducting long-term strategic planning and attempting to create anticipatory government (Fuerth, 2006). However, the turnover and shifts in priorities that accompany successive administrations can render this process difficult. Long-term planning, to the extent that it can be carried out at all, is necessarily limited to 2 or 4 years out. Strategies that take longer to achieve may be discarded by future administrations or congresses. Furthermore, policy planners must, in order to remain relevant, tailor their strategies based on the political priorities of the President under whom they serve.

Yet another challenge to long-term planning is the loss of institutional memory that accompanies personnel turnover. In federal organizations, most of the organization's institutional memory is held within the memories and experiences of its employees, and much of it will thus be lost with administration changes, regardless of the quality of transition teams.

While it will not formulate tactics itself, the Center will seek to provide a consistent basis for the creation of forward-thinking interagency grand strategy. This is to be accomplished by providing long-term projections and assessment of the global environment spanning well beyond the time frame of one administration. These projections will be continually assessed and revised, but they will retain the characteristics of incorporating all facets of national power. The work of the Center will thus help inform the policies of each new administration. As such, it will help minimize the risk that successive administrations will adopt narrow national priorities that fail to adequately understand the full range of issues, and it will continually remind policymakers of the long-term global environment. It also provides workshops and seminars, as well as a long-term strategic planning capability to maintain unity of purpose over successive administrations and generations of leadership.

In addition to providing forward-thinking visions to assist in policymaking, it can also serve as the memory of the bureaucracy for each new administration. It will enable new administrations to learn about past treaties, commitments, views, and processes that have occurred across the interagency.

By engaging all facets of national power and a full range of expertise to engage in short-, mid-, and long-term assessments of the global environment, the Center will enable the country to not only react to the changing global environment, but also to preempt changes to that environment and play an active role in shaping a better future through the development and use of scenarios and various other tools.

The Center will support the EOP in the development of whole-of-government grand strategies that are both long term (at least a decade) and interagency. The Center will provide national assessments of both geographical and functional threats and opportunities spanning the concentric and inclusive spectrums of space, the planet, specific regions and/or sub-regions, specific countries within regions, and the United States.

A National Security Strategic Management Process.

Developing grand strategies, either at the request of the President, the National Security Advisor, or any interagency issue team, will occur through the use of a generic strategic process to think through the policies and strategies that will be required to be developed. Issues that are strategic are not just important; the word "strategic" has at least two additional meanings. First, strategic issues are systemic, that is, they are related to an entire system and must be put into context. Second, strategic issues need to be dealt with over time, so all strategic issues have a temporal component to them as well. Since management is the process of directing the accomplishment of objectives through others, strategic management can be viewed as managing an institution as a system over time. The Center will always be looking out at least 10 years and will frequently study longer time horizons.

In the coming years, the new national strategies will need to be developed within the context of the world. The Center will support the integration of the nation's grand strategies based on pragmatic assessments and aspirational visions of what the future could be. The majority of the staff would be full-time civil servants, to provide continuity between administrations. The center would have many functions; assessment studies for the development of grand strategies, scenario development and gaming, outreach through conferences and projects, and "challenging conformist thinking," like Singapore.

CONCLUSIONS

In summary, the Center's core capabilities need to include:

- Strategic and systems thinking and "visioning,"
- The development of a holistic and evolving view of the global environment and national security context,
- The ability to game specific scenarios to assist in the formulation of contingency plans and to test the impacts of proposed policies,
- Regular development of scenarios out 10, 20, 50+ years,
- The capacity to house leading edge tools and technologies for assessments, especially "system risk,"
- Engaging in "red teaming" and alternative analyses to test assumptions and solutions with rigorous problem analysis,
- Providing, when necessary, classified research environments, developing grand strategies as assigned by the President, facilitating long-term planning, and preserving institutional memory,
- Providing networking and outreach to government, academia, industry and the general public, including public seminars and conferences,
- Challenging conventional wisdom in the Singaporean sense and the Project on National Security Reform sense.

The Center should be established to help senior government policymakers plan for the future and the role the United States will play in that future, including how the Nation will remain strong in the Marshall sense.

The entire world expects the United States to remain a leader. But, the United States cannot do this unless it is strong. It cannot be strong unless it plans for and shapes its future. The saying from the Judeo Christian Bible, "Where there is no vision, the people will perish," from Proverbs 29:18, is as true today as it was thousands of years ago.

As a nation, the United States needs to become proactive in using foresight and vision in shaping the future and working toward a world of increasing liberty, prosperity, justice, and peace because that is what future generations deserve.

REFERENCES

Benner, P. (2007, September). Vision Working Group Workshops, Project on National Security Reform, Washington, DC.

De Gues, A. (1997). The Living Company: Habits for Survival in a Turbulent Business Environment. Boston, MA: Harvard Business School Press.

Deming, W. E. (2000). The New Economics for Industry, Government Education (2nd Ed.), Boston, MA: MIT Press.

Eisenhower, Dwight D. Speech to the National Defense Executive Reserve Conference in Washington, DC (November 14, 1957), in *Public Papers of the Presidents of the United States, Dwight D. Eisenhower, 1957*, National Archives and Records Service, Washington, DC: U.S. Government Printing Office, p. 818.

I tell this story to illustrate the truth of the statement I heard long ago in the Army: *Plans are worthless, but planning is everything*. There is a very great distinction because when you are planning for an emergency you must start with this one thing: the very definition of 'emergency' is that it is unexpected; therefore, it is not going to happen the way you are planning.

Fuerth, L. S. (2006). Project on Forward Engagement. Washington, DC: George Washington University.

Ho, P. (2010). Thinking about the future: What the civil service can do. *Ethos,* Issue 7, Centre for Governance and Leadership, Civil Service College, Singapore.

Kugler, R. L. (2006). Policy Analysis in National Security Affairs: New Methods for a New Era. Washington, DC: Center for Technology and National Security Policy, National Defense University Press.

Lempert, R. (2007). "Can scenarios help policymakers be both bold and careful?" in F. Fukuyama (ed.), *Blindside: How to Anticipate Forcing Events and Wild Cards in Global Politics.* Baltimore, MD: Brookings Institution Press.

Marshall, G. C. (1945). *The winning of the war in Europe and the Pacific: Biennial report of the chief of staff of the United States Army, July 1, 1943, to June 30, 1945, to the secretary of war.* New York: Simon & Schuster.

Project on National Security Reform (2008). Forging a New Shield. Arlington, VA: Project on National Security Reform.

Ronis, S. R. (ed.) (2010). Project on National Security Reform Vision Working Group Report and Scenarios. Carlisle, PA: Strategic Studies Institute, U.S. Army War College.

Tzu, S. (1963). *The Art of War,* translated by Samuel B. Griffith, Oxford, England: Oxford University Press.

CHAPTER 10

POSTSCRIPT

Dr. Sheila R. Ronis

The Nation needs an ability to conduct grand strategy in the 21st century. But what does grand strategy mean in a large complex system? Perhaps we should consider a framework for the development of grand strategy — one that considers questions more than answers, system characteristics over specific functions, and organizing principles over rigid rules.

In a complex world of globalization, 21st century grand strategy is about thinking differently. It is about the relationships between economics, politics, progress (social, religious, cultural, technological), and physical, environmental, and national security systems, as well as interdependencies. It is a set of guidelines and concepts, as opposed to one idea, like "containment." Today's world has the West playing chess, a game of taking out the opponent while the East plays Igo, Weiqi, and Baduk — games of gaining and controlling ground. These ancient strategy games represent the difference between Sun Tzu and Clausewitz, perhaps an appropriate way of thinking in the new world. While the East thinks about winning a victory without firing a shot, by being smarter rather than winning and by being bigger, Westerners win by force. Although ancient, these games represent two worldviews and the kinds of challenges facing policymakers who must also develop grand strategy in a nonlinear construct.

In addition to new ways of thinking, complex systems knowledge is added that is critical to winning the grand strategy global competitions of the 21st century. Complexity science needs to inform policy and ultimately, grand strategy. Exploring complex system characteristics and organizing principles may be the best method to develop grand strategy in a world of complexity. Perhaps, this was the most important lesson learned from the symposium.

ABOUT THE CONTRIBUTORS

SHEILA R. RONIS is Professor and Chair, Department of Management and Communications at Walsh College in Troy, Michigan, where she teaches in the Doctorate and MBA Programs. She is also President of The University Group, Inc., a management consulting firm and think tank specializing in strategic management, visioning, national security, and public policy. A Fulbright Specialist Scholar, Dr. Ronis is studying the need for the development of grand strategy and foresight mechanisms in the Executive Office of the President of the United States. She is a Senior Advisor to Ambassador David Abshire at the Center for the Study of the Presidency and Congress. In December 2011, *Economic Security: Neglected Dimension of National Security*, published by National Defense University Press and edited by Dr. Ronis, was published based on a conference she chaired at NDU in August 2010. Dr. Ronis was a Distinguished Fellow and Vision Working Group leader of the congressionally mandated Project on National Security Reform (PNSR) in Washington. After nearly 40 years of working in government, industry, academia, and as the CEO of a management consulting firm, Dr. Ronis published *Timelines into the Future: Strategic Visioning Methods for Government, Industry and Other Organizations* (Hamilton Books, June 2007). She edited the *Project on National Security Reform Vision Working Group Report and Scenarios* (Strategic Studies Institute, U.S. Army War College, July 2010). In June, 2005, she chaired, at the Industrial College of the Armed Forces, the Army's Eisenhower National Security Series Conference, "The State of the U.S. Industrial Base: National Security Implications in a World of Globalization." The proceedings of that conference, which Dr. Ronis co-edited with Dr. Lynne Thompson, was published by the NDU Press in April 2006. In March, 2006, she completed a study of the national security implications of the erosion of the U.S. industrial base for the U.S. House of Representatives' Committee on Small Business. Dr. Ronis holds a B.S. in physics and mathematics, and an M.A. and Ph.D. in large social system behavior from Ohio State University.

DAVID M. ABSHIRE served as Assistant Secretary of State for Congressional Relations from 1970 to 1973 and worked out the plan that saved Radio Free Europe and Radio Liberty from extinction. In 1974, he was asked to become the first chairman of the Board for International Broadcasting. He was a member of the Murphy Commission on the Organization of the Government, the President's Foreign Intelligence Advisory Board, and the President's Task Force on U.S. Government International Broadcasting. During the transition of government in 1980, Dr. Abshire was asked by President-elect Ronald Reagan to head the National Security Group, which included the State and Defense Departments, the U.S. Information Agency, and the Central Intelligence Agency. He has also served on the Advisory Board of the Naval War College and on the Executive Panel of the Chief of Naval Operations. More recently, from 1983 to 1987, he was Ambassador to the North Atlantic Treaty Organization (NATO) where, in reaction to the threat posed by Soviet SS-20 missiles, he was the U.S. point man in Europe for deployment of Pershing and cruise missiles. It was this NATO success that convinced the Soviets to sign the historic Intermediate Range Nuclear Forces Treaty and withdraw their missiles. Ambassador Abshire initiated a new conventional defense improvement effort so that NATO would not have to rely heavily on nuclear weapons. In December 1986, at the depths of the Iran-Contra crisis, he was called by President Reagan to leave NATO to serve in his Cabinet and help restore confidence in the Presidency. He coordinated the Tower Board and the Independent Counsel. Dr. Abshire is the author of seven books: *The South Rejects a Prophet* (1967), *International Broadcasting: A New Dimension of Western Diplomacy* (1976), *Foreign Policy Makers: President vs. Congress* (1979), *Preventing World War III: A Realistic Grand Strategy* (1988), *Putting America's House in Order: The Nation as a Family* with Brock Brower (1996), *Saving the Reagan Presidency: Trust Is the Coin of the Realm* (2005), and *A Call to Greatness: Challenging Our Next President* (2008). He also wrote an essay for the Fetzer Institute's "Deepening the American Dream" series titled *The Grace and Power of Civility: Commitment and Tolerance in the American Tradition* (2004). He is editor of *Triumphs and Tragedies of the Modern Presidency: Seventy-Six Case Studies on Presidential Leadership* (2002), and author of CSPC publications: *The Character of George Washington* (1999), *Lessons For The 21st Century: Vulnerability and Surprise December 7, 1941 and September 11, 2001* (2002), and *The Character of George Marshall* (2005).

EVAN M. H. FABER is the Executive Associate for the Project on Forward Engagement and Special Assistant to Leon Fuerth. The Project on Forward Engagement promotes the use of anticipatory governance to improve the federal policy process by incorporating foresight as an actionable component of the policy process; networked systems to support whole-of-government responsiveness; and feedback systems to monitor performance and speed up learning from results. Mr. Faber is also cofounder and Acting Director of *Banaa. org,* an organization that connects talented Sudanese survivors of war with scholarship opportunities in the United States, as well as the tools and contacts to implement peace-promoting development strategies in their homeland. Mr. Faber holds a bachelor's degree in philosophy and designed a concentration in security, complexity, and foresight studies for a master's degree in international science and technology policy, both from the George Washington University.

PETER D. FEAVER is a Professor of Political Science and Public Policy at Duke University. He is Director of the Triangle Institute for Security Studies and Director of the Duke Program in American Grand Strategy. From June 2005 to July 2007, Dr. Feaver was on leave to be Special Advisor for Strategic Planning and Institutional Reform on the National Security Council Staff at the White House, where his responsibilities included the National Security Strategy, regional strategy reviews, and other political-military issues. In 1993-94, he served as Director for Defense Policy and Arms Control on the National Security Council at the White House, where his responsibilities included the *National Security Strategy* review, counterproliferation policy, regional nuclear arms control, and other defense policy issues. He is a member of the Aspen Strategy Group, blogs at *shadow.foreignpolicy.com,* and is a Contributing Editor to Foreign Policy magazine. Dr. Feaver is author of *Armed Servants: Agency, Oversight, and Civil-Military Relations* (Harvard Press, 2003) and *Guarding the Guardians: Civilian Control of Nuclear Weapons in the United States* (Cornell University Press, 1992). He is co-author, with Christopher Gelpi and

Jason Reifler, of *Paying the Human Costs of War* (Princeton University Press, 2009); with Susan Wasiolek and Anne Crossman, of *Getting the Most Out of College* (Ten Speed Press, 2008); and with Christopher Gelpi, of *Choosing Your Battles: American Civil-Military Relations and the Use of Force* (Princeton University Press, 2004). He is co-editor, with Richard H. Kohn, of *Soldiers and Civilians: The Civil-Military Gap and American National Security* (MIT Press, 2001). He has published numerous other monographs, scholarly articles, book chapters, and policy pieces on American foreign policy, public opinion, nuclear proliferation, civil-military relations, information warfare, and U.S. national security. Dr. Ferber holds a Ph.D. from Harvard University.

LEON S. FUERTH is the Founder and Director of the Project on Forward Engagement, Distinguished Research Fellow at the National Defense University, Research Professor of International Affairs at the George Washington University, and the former National Security Advisor to Vice President Al Gore. During the Bill Clinton administration, Mr. Fuerth served simultaneously on the Deputies' and Principals' Committees of the National Security Council, created and managed five binational commissions, and led efforts to develop the International Space Station; marshal international support for sanctions against Slobodan Milosevic's regime; take action to prevent the spread of HIV/AIDS in Africa; denuclearize former Soviet states; win China's cooperation in protecting the environment and reducing pollution; and spur foreign investment in Egypt as part of the Middle East peace process. The Project on Forward Engagement promotes the use of Anticipatory Governance to improve the federal policy process by incorporating: foresight as an actionable component of the policy process; networked systems to support whole-of-government responsiveness; and feedback systems to monitor performance and speed up learning from results. The Project is funded by the MacArthur foundation and operates simultaneously at the National Defense University and the George Washington University. Mr. Fuerth holds a bachelor's degree in English and a master's degree in history from New York University, and a master's degree in public administration from Harvard University.

ALLEN S. MILLER is an experienced strategist, analyst, and educator serving as a Deputy Assistant Director for the Office of Risk Management and Analysis in the National Protection and Programs Directorate of the Department of Homeland Security in Washington, DC. In this capacity, Dr. Miller is responsible for directing a team of professionals working to enable and advance a unified approach to managing risk to our homeland, leveraging the capabilities of all the components of the homeland security enterprise, including federal, state, local, tribal, and territorial government organizations, the private sector, and our international partners. As a U.S. Government civil servant for over 30 years, Dr. Miller has served in multiple positions with varying degrees of responsibility at the Central Intelligence Agency, the U.S. Air Force Defense Mapping Agency Aerospace Center, the U.S. Army Test and Evaluation Agency, the U.S. Army War College, and the U.S. Coast Guard. Dr. Miller holds a bachelor of science degree and a master of public administration degree from the Pennsylvania State University, is a graduate of the U.S. Army War College Strategic Studies program, and holds a doctor of philosophy degree in education from Walden University.

ROBERT B. POLK has served in various senior level planning and execution management positions both in and out of government. Today, he remains a Senior Adjunct Research Member and Consultant with the Institute for Defense Analyses in Washington, DC, where his ongoing experience helping develop such capacity in several U.S. Departments continues to provide valuable insights. He recently completed 3 years as Senior Advisor, Strategic Planner, Deputy Issue Team Lead, and cofounding member of PNSR. Previous experiences were during his 20-year military career as both a front lines combat infantry officer and senior civil-military strategist for major Army and multiservice commands serving across the international spectrum from Thailand to Japan, Bosnia, Germany, and Iraq, including many months as the Co-Creator and Co-Director of the Office of Policy Planning to the United Nations-sanctioned Coalition Provisional Authority under Ambassador L. Paul Bremer in the early days of Iraq. Preceding this, Mr. Polk served as the Director of Plans for the original U.S. civil-military coordination team going into Baghdad called the Office of Reconstruction and Humanitarian Assistance led by Lieutenant General (Ret.) Jay Garner. A West Point graduate, Mr. Polk holds a master of military arts and science in operational theory and strategic planning from the Army's premier School of Advanced Military Studies, and a master of arts in national security and strategic studies from the U.S. Naval War College.

CYNTHIA A. WATSON is Professor of Security at the National War College. She served for 5 years as Associate Dean for Academic Affairs, then Associate Dean for Curriculum and Faculty Development. She also served as the Chairwoman of the Naval War College's Department of Security Studies and Director of the Electives Program, and as a core course director. Prior positions included Assistant Dean for Social Sciences and Assistant Professor in the Department of Political Science at Loyola University Chicago and Assistant Professor of Politics at Ithaca College. Additionally, Dr. Watson has worked for the U.S. General Accounting Office and U.S. House of Representatives. Dr. Watson also served as Senior Advisor to the Society for International Business Fellows' New Member Program from 2006 to 2010. An active speaker and author, she has been named University of Missouri-Kansas City's Alumna of the Year 2011. She is on the Governing Boards of a number of professional organizations and the Editorial Board of *Third World Quarterly*, along with being a Member of the International Institute for Strategic Studies and the Society for Military History. Her current research interests include China-Taiwan in Latin America and China's security concerns in its new world posture. Her first edition (2002) of *U.S. National Security* received CHOICE's designation as a Book of the Year. Other publications include *Nation-Building, U.S. Military Service, Military Education, and U.S. National Security* (2nd Ed.), *Political Role of the Military* (co-edited with Constantine Danopoulos), and *Interest Groups in National Security; and Combatant Commands: Origins, Structure, and Engagements* (Praeger, 2011). She is also completing a manuscript on nation-building/stability operations for Praeger Security International. Dr. Watson holds a B.A., with honors, from the University of Missouri at Kansas City, an M.A. from the London School of Economics, and a Ph.D. from the University of Notre Dame.

www.ingramcontent.com/pod-product-compliance
Lightning Source LLC
Chambersburg PA
CBHW060150300526
45790CB00014B/430